Innovation

The Hidden Windrush Legacy for Generational Wealth

by
Dr. Sonia Michelle Reynolds

Table of Contents

journey toward a prosperous future often begins with the courage to embark on a path of uncertainty, guided by the light of hope.

The Historical Context

In the aftermath of World War II, the world was a canvas of destruction, yet pregnant with the possibility of rebirth and renewal. The British Empire, though victorious, was grappling with the extensive damage inflicted upon its infrastructure and economy. It was within this landscape of devastation and hope that the voyage of the Windrush must be understood—a journey not merely of physical translocation but of profound historical significance.

The conception of the Windrush voyage was catalyzed by a multitude of exigencies. Britain's labor market was in dire straits, with gaping wounds in its workforce that needed immediate attention. The colonies of the British Empire, with their reservoirs of able-bodied individuals, presented a promising solution to this quandary. The Windrush, therefore, symbolized not merely a ship but a vessel of hope both for Britain in its quest for reconstruction and for the passengers it carried, who were in pursuit of a new beginning.

It is essential to reckon with the socio-political milieu from which the Windrush set sail. The Caribbean, embroiled in its own complexities post-World War II, was a region where the glimmers of independence were beginning to spark amidst the ashes of colonial rule. For many inhabitants, the Windrush journey represented an escape from economic stagnation and

Unveiling the Legacy

In the grand tapestry of history, the Windrush generation marks an indelible chapter, embodying hope, resilience, and the indomitable human spirit. This book aims to shine a light on the profound legacy left by this generation, exploring not just their journey but how they laid the foundations for future generations to build their paths towards prosperity and well-being. The Windrush saga, stretching from the thrilling voyage for a better life to the enduring challenges and triumphs, reveals a story of perseverance that continues to inspire and guide us today.

Their arrival on British shores was not just a moment in time but a catalyst that transformed societies, economies, and cultures. This narrative delves deep into the Windrush generation's contributions, far beyond the temporal confines of their initial landing. From bolstering the British economy to enriching its cultural landscape, their impact is profound and multifaceted. By weaving through the threads of history, this work lays bare the concepts of generational wealth, the spirit of innovation, and the relentless pursuit of progress that characterized their journey and those who followed.

Amidst the backdrop of adversity, the Windrush generation's story is one of creativity and entrepreneurial spirit, chiseling out a space for future generations in a landscape that was often unwelcoming. This book serves as a beacon of hope, illustrating how the legacies left by past generations can fuel the ambitions and dreams of the present and future. Through a meticulous chronicling of their contributions, struggles, and unyielding resilience, "Unveiling the Legacy" invites readers to reflect on the past with an eye towards forging a prosperous and inclusive future for all. It is an homage to the enduring impact of the Windrush generation and a roadmap for leveraging the power of innovation, education, and unity in the journey towards achieving lasting wealth and well-being.

Chapter 1:
The Windrush Voyage: A Journ
Hope Charting New Horizor

Within the tapestry of time, there are mc define generations, sculpting the future decisions and sacrifices of the past. Among th events, the voyage of the Empire Windrush stands of hope and a testament to human resilience. In 194 embarked from the Caribbean to the United Kir decks brimming not with goods, but with souls seek beginning amidst the ruins of post-war Britain. Th was not embarked upon lightly; it was fueled by a con of excitement and hope, a potent mixture that compe individuals to leave their homes behind in search of p and fulfillment. The passengers of Windrush were n travelers; they were pioneers in their own right, armed relentless spirit to overcome and the unwavering ho their journey would sow the seeds for generational wea well-being. In navigating the tumultuous waters of c they laid the cornerstone for future generations, provir from the depths of hardship can emerge unbreakable st and enduring legacies. The story of the Windrush voyag powerful narrative of transformation, a vivid reminder th the vestiges of imperial domination, toward the promise of prosperity and autonomy.

However, the journey of the Windrush and its passengers cannot be romantically idealized. The voyage was underpinned by hope, a testament to the resilience of those who dared to dream. The passengers aboard the Windrush were not merely moving geographically; they were navigating the chasms of racial, economic, and social divides that they would confront upon their arrival in Britain.

The British government's invitation to the Windrush passengers was laced with paradoxes. It was a beckoning for aid in rebuilding a motherland that many of its colonial subjects had never seen, to repair the vestiges of devastation that they had not wrought. This acknowledgment is crucial in comprehending the complexities that awaited the Windrush generation upon their arrival.

Upon setting foot on British soil, the Windrush passengers embarked on a journey of relentless challenges and resilience. They were confronted with the cold visage of xenophobia, racism, and a plethora of social and economic barriers. Yet, their determination to carve out a space for themselves in a land that was equally foreign as it was promised played a pivotal role in the cultural and economic tapestry of post-war Britain.

The significance of the Windrush voyage extends beyond the narratives of struggle; it is a story of monumental contributions and the indomitable spirit of a generation that sowed the seeds of diversity and multiculturalism in British society. The contributions of the Windrush generation to Britain's cultural, social, and economic landscapes are inextricable from the narrative of post-war reconstruction and the evolution of British identity.

In understanding the historical context of the Windrush voyage, one must also appreciate the broader implications of the migration patterns it heralded. The Windrush voyage was not an isolated event but a precursor to a series of migrations that would reshuffle the demographic and cultural compositions of many Western nations. It signaled the beginning of a global movement towards understanding and embracing multiculturalism as a cornerstone of modern society.

The journey of the Windrush is a narrative replete with lessons on the complexities of nationality, belonging, and identity. It underscores the profound impacts of historical events on generations and highlights the enduring human quest for dignity, acceptance, and opportunity. The Windrush voyage, therefore, is not just a chapter in British history but a testament to the resilience and transformative power of the human spirit.

As we delve further into the legacies of the Windrush generation, it is imperative to recognize the intricate web of historical, social, and economic factors that shaped their experiences. Their journey underscores the importance of viewing history not as a series of isolated events but as interconnected narratives that continue to influence the present and future.

Unveiling the Legacy

In the grand tapestry of history, the Windrush generation marks an indelible chapter, embodying hope, resilience, and the indomitable human spirit. This book aims to shine a light on the profound legacy left by this generation, exploring not just their journey but how they laid the foundations for future generations to build their paths towards prosperity and well-being. The Windrush saga, stretching from the thrilling voyage for a better life to the enduring challenges and triumphs, reveals a story of perseverance that continues to inspire and guide us today.

Their arrival on British shores was not just a moment in time but a catalyst that transformed societies, economies, and cultures. This narrative delves deep into the Windrush generation's contributions, far beyond the temporal confines of their initial landing. From bolstering the British economy to enriching its cultural landscape, their impact is profound and multifaceted. By weaving through the threads of history, this work lays bare the concepts of generational wealth, the spirit of innovation, and the relentless pursuit of progress that characterized their journey and those who followed.

Amidst the backdrop of adversity, the Windrush generation's story is one of creativity and entrepreneurial spirit, chiseling out a space for future generations in a landscape that was often unwelcoming. This book serves as a beacon of hope, illustrating how the legacies left by past generations can fuel the ambitions and dreams of the present and future. Through a meticulous chronicling of their contributions, struggles, and unyielding resilience, "Unveiling the Legacy" invites readers to reflect on the past with an eye towards forging a prosperous and inclusive future for all. It is an homage to the enduring impact of the Windrush generation and a roadmap for leveraging the power of innovation, education, and unity in the journey towards achieving lasting wealth and well-being.

Chapter 1:
The Windrush Voyage: A Journey of Hope Charting New Horizons

Within the tapestry of time, there are moments that define generations, sculpting the future with the decisions and sacrifices of the past. Among these pivotal events, the voyage of the Empire Windrush stands as a beacon of hope and a testament to human resilience. In 1948, the ship embarked from the Caribbean to the United Kingdom, its decks brimming not with goods, but with souls seeking a new beginning amidst the ruins of post-war Britain. This journey was not embarked upon lightly; it was fueled by a combination of excitement and hope, a potent mixture that compelled these individuals to leave their homes behind in search of prosperity and fulfillment. The passengers of Windrush were not mere travelers; they were pioneers in their own right, armed with the relentless spirit to overcome and the unwavering hope that their journey would sow the seeds for generational wealth and well-being. In navigating the tumultuous waters of change, they laid the cornerstone for future generations, proving that from the depths of hardship can emerge unbreakable strength and enduring legacies. The story of the Windrush voyage is a powerful narrative of transformation, a vivid reminder that the journey toward a prosperous future often begins with the courage to embark on a path of uncertainty, guided by the light of hope.

The Historical Context

In the aftermath of World War II, the world was a canvas of destruction, yet pregnant with the possibility of rebirth and renewal. The British Empire, though victorious, was grappling with the extensive damage inflicted upon its infrastructure and economy. It was within this landscape of devastation and hope that the voyage of the Windrush must be understood—a journey not merely of physical translocation but of profound historical significance.

The conception of the Windrush voyage was catalyzed by a multitude of exigencies. Britain's labor market was in dire straits, with gaping wounds in its workforce that needed immediate attention. The colonies of the British Empire, with their reservoirs of able-bodied individuals, presented a promising solution to this quandary. The Windrush, therefore, symbolized not merely a ship but a vessel of hope both for Britain in its quest for reconstruction and for the passengers it carried, who were in pursuit of a new beginning.

It is essential to reckon with the socio-political milieu from which the Windrush set sail. The Caribbean, embroiled in its own complexities post-World War II, was a region where the glimmers of independence were beginning to spark amidst the ashes of colonial rule. For many inhabitants, the Windrush journey represented an escape from economic stagnation and the vestiges of imperial domination, toward the promise of prosperity and autonomy.

However, the journey of the Windrush and its passengers cannot be romantically idealized. The voyage was underpinned by hope, a testament to the resilience of those who dared to dream. The passengers aboard the Windrush were not merely moving geographically; they were navigating the chasms of racial, economic, and social divides that they would confront upon their arrival in Britain.

The British government's invitation to the Windrush passengers was laced with paradoxes. It was a beckoning for aid in rebuilding a motherland that many of its colonial subjects had never seen, to repair the vestiges of devastation that they had not wrought. This acknowledgment is crucial in comprehending the complexities that awaited the Windrush generation upon their arrival.

Upon setting foot on British soil, the Windrush passengers embarked on a journey of relentless challenges and resilience. They were confronted with the cold visage of xenophobia, racism, and a plethora of social and economic barriers. Yet, their determination to carve out a space for themselves in a land that was equally foreign as it was promised played a pivotal role in the cultural and economic tapestry of post-war Britain.

The significance of the Windrush voyage extends beyond the narratives of struggle; it is a story of monumental contributions and the indomitable spirit of a generation that sowed the seeds of diversity and multiculturalism in British society. The contributions of the Windrush generation to Britain's cultural, social, and economic landscapes are inextricable from the narrative of post-war reconstruction and the evolution of British identity.

In understanding the historical context of the Windrush voyage, one must also appreciate the broader implications of the migration patterns it heralded. The Windrush voyage was not an isolated event but a precursor to a series of migrations that would reshuffle the demographic and cultural compositions of many Western nations. It signaled the beginning of a global movement towards understanding and embracing multiculturalism as a cornerstone of modern society.

The journey of the Windrush is a narrative replete with lessons on the complexities of nationality, belonging, and identity. It underscores the profound impacts of historical events on generations and highlights the enduring human quest for dignity, acceptance, and opportunity. The Windrush voyage, therefore, is not just a chapter in British history but a testament to the resilience and transformative power of the human spirit.

As we delve further into the legacies of the Windrush generation, it is imperative to recognize the intricate web of historical, social, and economic factors that shaped their experiences. Their journey underscores the importance of viewing history not as a series of isolated events but as interconnected narratives that continue to influence the present and future.

The voyage of the Windrush encapsulates a pivotal moment in history where the past and future converged, where the ashes of war gave birth to new possibilities. It is a narrative that embodies the interplay of hope and desperation, of rebuilding and discovery, and most importantly, the indelible impact of a generation that dared to dream amidst adversity.

Therefore, as we reflect on the historical context of the Windrush voyage, we must do so with a deep sense of reverence and a commitment to draw inspiration from its legacy. It is a call to recognize the power of resilience, cultural exchange, and the relentless pursuit of prosperity and wellbeing. The Windrush generation's journey from hope and desperation to enduring legacy serves as a beacon, illuminating the path towards a future where diversity and inclusion are not just accepted but celebrated as pillars of strength.

In embracing the lessons of the Windrush voyage, we are reminded of the undeniable truth that our collective histories, no matter how fraught with adversity, are potent sources of inspiration and empowerment. The historical context of the Windrush voyage is not just a narrative of the past; it is a living, breathing legacy that continues to shape the contours of our present and future.

Thus, the story of the Windrush is a clarion call to all - to honor the past, to cherish the contributions of those who came before us, and to forge ahead with hope and determination towards creating a world that truly values and uplifts every individual. In this light, the voyage of the Windrush transcends the annals of history to become a perennial source of inspiration and a testament to the unyielding strength of the human spirit.

World War II and the British Empire World War II was a pivotal moment in the history of the British Empire, profoundly impacting its global standing and initiating irreversible changes that would shape the future of its colonial territories, particularly in the Caribbean. The war not only drained Britain's economic and military resources but also exposed the vulnerabilities of the empire, leading to a reevaluation of its colonial policies and relationships with its territories.

The necessity for manpower during the war led to thousands of Caribbean citizens answering Britain's call to arms. They served valiantly in various capacities, from pilots in the Royal Air Force to workers in munition factories. Their contribution was not just a demonstration of loyalty to the 'Mother Country' but also a fight for the ideals of freedom and democracy against the tyranny of fascism. This participation was a crucible that forged a new sense of identity and purpose among the Caribbean populations, igniting aspirations for greater autonomy and rights.

As the war concluded, the British Empire, weakened and indebted, could no longer maintain its grip on its colonies with the same rigor as before. The empire's decline was hastened by the rise of anti-colonial movements across the world, including in the Caribbean. These movements were buoyed by the returning servicemen and women who, having fought for freedom overseas, were now determined to seek it at home. Their experiences and newly acquired skills would become invaluable in the struggle for independence and self-determination.

The end of World War II also marked the beginning of a massive reconstruction effort in Britain. The country was in desperate need of labor to rebuild its shattered economy and infrastructure. This need would lead to the British Nationality Act of 1948, which granted citizenship and the right of settlement in the UK to all British colonial subjects. This legislation set the stage for the Windrush generation's journey to Britain, transforming the social and cultural landscape of the nation.

However, the transition was not without its challenges. The Windrush settlers, notwithstanding their contributions during the war, faced a Britain that was often cold, both meteorologically and socially. They encountered prejudice, discrimination, and a lack of understanding from the very society they had fought to protect. Yet, their resilience and determination to succeed, coupled with their innovative spirit, saw them make significant contributions to British society, from labor and healthcare to culture and politics.

The legacy of the Windrush generation is a testimony to the enduring human spirit's capacity to overcome adversity. Their journey from the Caribbean to Britain, driven in part by the seismic shifts caused by World War II, reshaped not only their lives but also the very fabric of British society. They laid the groundwork for future generations to pursue prosperity and fulfilment, challenging the barriers of race, class, and ethnicity.

Furthermore, the narrative of the Windrush generation highlights the interconnectedness of the British Empire's history with the personal stories of its colonial subjects. It illustrates how global events can have profound, far-reaching impacts on individuals and communities, steering the course of their destinies in unexpected ways.

In the aftermath of World War II, as the British Empire receded into history, it left behind a legacy of transformation and change. The Windrush generation, as part of this legacy, stands as a beacon of hope and resilience, inspiring not only their descendants but all who seek to build a better future amidst the challenges of an ever-changing world.

The story of the Windrush generation is not just about the past; it is a continuing journey of hope, innovation, and triumph over adversity. It serves as a powerful reminder of the contributions migrants have made to Britain and the importance of embracing diversity and inclusion for a prosperous society. As we look to the future, the Windrush legacy offers invaluable lessons on resilience, innovation, and the pursuit of generational wealth and wellbeing.

In conclusion, World War II was a turning point for the British Empire and its Caribbean colonies. It catalyzed a series of events that would lead to significant demographic, social, and economic changes in Britain. The Windrush generation, borne out of this tumultuous period, embodied the values of perseverance, adaptability, and commitment to community, setting a precedent for future generations to follow. Their legacy is a testament to the power of hope and the enduring nature of the human spirit in the face of adversity, guiding us towards a brighter, more inclusive future.

The Arrival and its Impact

The arrival of the Windrush at the Tilbury Docks on June 22, 1948, marked a pivotal moment in British history. Aboard the ship were hundreds of hopeful souls from the Caribbean, each with dreams of prosperity and a better life in what they considered the Mother Country. This moment didn't just signify the physical journey across the Atlantic but also symbolized a monumental shift in the social and economic fabric of post-war Britain.

The welcoming of the Windrush passengers was met with a mixture of anticipation and apprehension. Britain, still reeling from the devastations of World War II, was in desperate need of rebuilding. The arrival of these passengers presented an opportunity for the nation to fill labor shortages in various sectors, from transportation to the newly established National Health Service. However, what wasn't fully anticipated was the societal impact their presence would bring.

The newcomers faced a harsh reality upon their arrival. Despite leaving behind their homes for promises of employment and acceptance, many encountered prejudice and exclusion. The initial warmth of reception by some was not universally shared, and the Windrush generation had to navigate a landscape that was often hostile and unwelcoming.

Yet, their impact on British society was undeniable. They brought with them a rich cultural heritage that soon began to weave itself into the fabric of British life. From the culinary flavors of the Caribbean to the rhythms of calypso and reggae, the Windrush generation started to shape a new cultural identity in Britain.

What's more, their contributions to the economy were substantial. As they filled labor shortages, they became an integral part of Britain's pathway to recovery and growth. Their work ethic, determination, and resilience were a boost to industries that had been struggling since the war's end. This economic contribution, though often underrecognized, helped lay the groundwork for the multicultural Britain we see today.

However, the journey of the Windrush generation wasn't without its trials. They faced considerable obstacles, from finding accommodation to confronting overt racism. Some adverts for housing openly stated, "No blacks, no Irish, no dogs," a stark reminder of the intolerance of the era. Despite these challenges, the Windrush migrants displayed remarkable fortitude, banding together to form tight-knit communities that provided mutual support and solidarity.

One can't overlook the impact on the British legal and political landscape. The arrival of the Windrush generation and their struggles with discrimination and civil rights issues catalyzed a series of legislative reforms. These reforms aimed to address racial discrimination and laid the foundations for Britain's race relations policies.

Furthermore, the Windrush generation's faith in the face of adversity served as a beacon of hope for future generations. They established churches, social clubs, and community organizations that not only served as sanctuaries of cultural preservation but also as platforms for activism and social change. Their legacy is one of resilience, which continues to inspire today.

As Britain evolved into a multicultural society, the influences of the Windrush generation became more deeply intertwined in the national consciousness. Their contributions went beyond the labor market, influencing arts, music, literature, and even the British lexicon.

However, their story is also a testament to the enduring spirit of hope. Despite the hurdles, the Windrush generation laid the foundations for future generations of Caribbean descent in Britain. Their struggles have paved the way for conversations about identity, belonging, and the importance of diversity and inclusion in shaping a more equitable society.

Their arrival also redefined the concept of Britishness. By contributing to the nation's recovery and cultural enrichment, they challenged preconceived notions of what it means to be British. The Windrush era, therefore, marks the beginning of a journey toward a more inclusive understanding of national identity, one that celebrates diversity as a strength.

This monumental impact underscores the significance of the Windrush generation in the annals of British history. Their story is a poignant reminder of the complexities of migration, the struggles against adversity, and the indomitable spirit of hope and resilience. It's a narrative that enriches the fabric of Britain, teaching invaluable lessons on tolerance, unity, and the power of diversity.

In reflecting on the Windrush's legacy, it's crucial to acknowledge the dual narrative of hardship and triumph that characterizes their experience. Their journey of hope and desperation has left an indelible mark on the nation, shaping modern Britain in ways that are still being understood and appreciated. The Windrush generation's contributions have become an integral part of the national story, a chapter that continues to inspire future generations to strive for success amidst adversity.

As we look to the future, the story of the Windrush serves as a powerful testament to the strength of the human spirit and the transformative power of migration. It offers a roadmap for understanding how unity in diversity can lead to a prosperous and inclusive society. The legacy of the Windrush generation endures as a beacon of hope, motivating us to build on their foundation of resilience, innovation, and determination to achieve generational wealth and wellbeing. Their journey, marked by both hope and desperation, continues to inspire us to envision a future where prosperity and fulfillment are within reach for all.

Chapter 2:
The West Indian Contribution:
Beyond the Shores

The narrative of the West Indian diaspora is not merely one of physical migration but a profound reshaping of cultural and economic landscapes far beyond their homelands. As we delve into the rich tapestry of the West Indian contribution, it becomes evident that their impact extends well into realms unforeseen at the onset of the Windrush voyage. This chapter illuminates how the perseverance, resilience, and indefatigable spirit of the West Indian immigrants have significantly shaped the societies they integrated into, especially the United Kingdom. Through their hard work in the foundational years following World War II, they played a crucial role in rebuilding the nation, contributing to various sectors such as public transport, the NHS, and manufacturing industries. But their influence didn't stop at economic revival; it echoed in the vibrant cultural contributions that have since become an inseparable part of Britain's identity. From the tantalizing flavors of Jerk cuisine to the pulsating rhythms of Reggae and Soca, West Indians infused a new life into the cultural milieu, fostering a rich environment of multiculturalism and diversity that challenged the status quo.

As we explore the multitude of ways in which the West Indian communities have contributed beyond mere labor, they emerge not only as architects of post-war Britain but also as harbingers of change, embodying a relentless quest for dignity, recognition, and prosperity. Their journey, fraught with challenges yet brimming with accomplishments, serves as a beacon of hope, showing that contributions to society go beyond economic metrics, enriching the social fabric and leaving an indelible mark on the heart and soul of nations.

Contributions to the British Economy

The West Indian contribution to the British economy is a vibrant narrative of resilience, innovation, and indomitable spirit. Post the Windrush voyage, the British Isles found themselves in a phase of reconstruction, a period marked by a pressing need for labor to rebuild what the war had ravaged. It was within this context that the West Indian immigrants stepped onto British soil, not just as seekers of better opportunities but as bearers of hope and a willingness to partake in the nation's recovery.

Their arrival signified the beginning of a transformative era in the British economic landscape. Initially, West Indian immigrants faced a barrage of challenges, from navigating societal prejudices to overcoming barriers in employment. Yet, their unwavering determination saw them gradually integrate into various sectors of the economy, notably in public transportation, the health sector, and manufacturing. This integration was not just a mere addition of numbers to the workforce but brought about a profound diversification of skills and perspectives, essential for innovation and growth.

In the health sector, for instance, the contribution of West Indian nurses was monumental. Hospitals across Britain were understaffed and overwhelmed, a situation exacerbated by the post-war baby boom and the onset of the National Health Service (NHS) in 1948. The recruitment of West Indian nurses not only filled this void but also instilled a new dynamism within the NHS, setting a precedent for multiculturalism in the workforce.

The public transportation system too witnessed a significant transformation, thanks to the West Indian workforce. London Transport, reeling from a shortage of manpower, launched recruitment drives in the Caribbean. The influx of West Indian workers revitalized the system, ensuring its efficiency and reliability, foundational elements for economic robustness and public welfare.

Furthermore, the impact of West Indian immigrants extended beyond filling labor shortages. They embodied an entrepreneurial spirit, setting up businesses that catered not only to the nostalgic tastes of the Caribbean community but also introduced the broader British populace to a diversity of flavors, sounds, and crafts. These enterprises, though small in scale, played a crucial role in weaving the fabric of a multicultural Britain and underscored the economic principle that diversity fuels innovation.

This narrative of economic contribution is incomplete without acknowledging the cultural capital West Indian immigrants brought. The richness of Caribbean culture, expressed through music, festivals, and cuisine, tremendously enriched British society. This cultural infusion not only augmented the quality of life but also stimulated the growth of creative industries within the UK, contributing significantly to the economy.

The presence of West Indian communities further facilitated trade relations between the Caribbean and the UK, opening markets for products that were unfamiliar in Britain before their arrival. This not only diversified the British market but also supported Caribbean economies, exemplifying a symbiotic relationship that transcends mere labor contribution.

The fiscal contributions through taxes and participation in the burgeoning consumer society of post-war Britain further underline the economic imprint of the West Indian diaspora. Their involvement in the workforce and entrepreneurial ventures contributed to the nation's exchequer, aiding public services and infrastructure development, crucial for a country in reconstruction.

On a broader scale, the adaptation and resilience demonstrated by the West Indian workforce inspired reforms in labor laws and practices, paving the way for more inclusive and diversified workplaces. Their journey accentuated the importance of equal opportunities, contributing to the gradual dismantling of discriminatory barriers, thereby fostering a more equitable labor market.

Education and professional development were other arenas where the West Indian influence was felt. Striving for upward mobility, they invested in education, both for themselves and their progeny, gradually populating professions that were hitherto less accessible. This progression not only altered the demographic composition of these sectors but also enriched them with fresh perspectives and vigor.

Moreover, the West Indian diaspora's participation in trade unions and collective bargaining contributed to the improvement of working conditions, wages, and workers' rights. Their struggle for equality and justice in the workplace had far-reaching implications, strengthening the labor movement in Britain.

In the realm of sports, individuals of West Indian descent have left an indelible mark, becoming symbols of excellence and unity. Their success stories, transcending racial and social barriers, have been a source of inspiration, illustrating the community's broader contributions beyond the economic sphere.

Iteratively, the West Indian diaspora has played a pivotal role in shaping the socio-economic landscape of Britain. Their journey, marked by challenges, perseverance, and triumphs, exemplifies the profound impact of migration on the development of a nation. It is a testament to the notion that the prosperity of a society is intrinsically linked to its inclusivity, diversity, and the collective endeavors of its people.

The legacy of the West Indian diaspora's contribution to the British economy is a beacon of hope and a blueprint for future generations. It underscores the invaluable role of migrants in fostering economic dynamism, cultural richness, and societal openness. As we look ahead, this legacy not only serves as a cornerstone of historical pride but also a guiding light for embracing diversity as a catalyst for prosperity and wellbeing.

Thus, the narrative of the West Indian contribution to the British economy is one of enduring significance. It is a narrative that transcends mere economic metrics, encapsulating a journey of resilience, cultural amalgamation, and an unwavering quest for progress and equality. In reflecting on this journey, it becomes evident that the prosperity of a nation lies not just in its economic wealth but in the richness of its diversity and the collective spirit of its people.

Rebuilding Post-War Britain In the aftermath of World War II, Britain faced a monumental task. Cities lay in ruins, industries were at a standstill, and the spirit of the British people was tested as never before. Amid this backdrop of destruction and uncertainty, a wave of hope arrived on the shores of Britain, embodied by the passengers of the Windrush. Their arrival marked a pivotal moment in Britain's journey towards reconstruction and prosperity.

The Windrush generation, initially invited to assist with the labor shortages in the post-war period, became instrumental in the rebuilding of Britain. They took on roles that were critical yet often overlooked, working in public transport, the newly formed National Health Service (NHS), and in the reconstruction of the nation's infrastructure. Their contributions were not merely in the filling of labor gaps; they introduced fresh perspectives and a resilience that became intertwined with the narrative of recovery.

This period of reconstruction also coincided with the beginning of a significant social transformation within Britain. The arrival of these immigrants from the Caribbean introduced a multicultural dimension to British society that had not previously existed on such a scale. This integration was not without its challenges, yet it laid the groundwork for the diverse and inclusive society that we witness today.

One should not underestimate the significance of this chapter in our shared history. The fabric of post-war Britain was woven with strands of perseverance, innovation, and a profound sense of hope brought forward by the Windrush generation. Their legacy, however, extends beyond the physical rebuilding of a nation. They planted the seeds for generational wealth, beginning with their tireless work ethic and the importance they placed on education and community.

The influence of this pioneering generation can be seen in the thriving West Indian businesses that began to take root during this time. These entrepreneurs faced numerous obstacles, yet their resilience and determination to succeed laid the foundation for economic empowerment and the creation of generational wealth within their communities.

They also brought with them a rich cultural heritage that has since become an intrinsic part of British culture. From food to music, the cultural contributions of the Windrush generation have enriched Britain's social fabric, fostering a spirit of creativity and innovation that has propelled the country into new eras of artistic and cultural growth.

As we reflect on this critical period of rebuilding and growth, it serves as a timeless reminder of the strength found in diversity and the transformative power of human potential. The Windrush generation's role in rebuilding post-war Britain is a profound illustration of how individuals, hailing from different corners of the globe, can come together to forge a brighter future out of the ruins of devastation.

The lessons learned during this period of reconstruction are as relevant today as they were then. They serve as a beacon of hope, highlighting the enduring legacy of the Windrush generation and offering a roadmap for future generations to achieve prosperity and fulfillment in both wealth and wellbeing. It is a testament to the indomitable spirit of those who, in the face of adversity, championed the values of hard work, innovation, and unity.

In contemplating this chapter of history, we are reminded of the importance of embracing diversity and the profound impact that a group of determined individuals can have on a nation's destiny. The story of the Windrush generation and their pivotal role in the rebuilding of post-war Britain is not just a tale of resilience and contribution; it is a narrative that continues to inspire and guide us towards creating a more inclusive, prosperous, and vibrant society for all.

Thus, as we move forward, let us carry with us the legacy of those who helped rebuild Britain. Let their journey motivate us to strive for excellence in our endeavors and to build bridges where there are divides. For in the lessons of the past lie the keys to our future, a future where the spirits of innovation, unity, and perseverance prevail in our continuous quest for generational wealth and wellbeing.

Cultural Fusion and Resistance

The journey of the Windrush generation, as they settled beyond the shores of the Caribbean, was not just a physical relocation but a remarkable saga of cultural fusion and resistance. This chapter aims to illuminate the vibrant tapestry woven by the West Indian diaspora, which not only enriched British society but also laid the groundwork for cultural resilience and identity defiance. As these courageous souls navigated the challenges of integration, they forged a legacy of diversity that continues to resonate.

In the wake of their arrival, the Windrush generation encountered a Britain that was, in many ways, unprepared for the richness and complexity of West Indian culture. Faced with an icy reception and systemic barriers, this community's response was neither to retreat nor to surrender their cultural heritage. Instead, they chose to stand tall, integrating their traditions with a determination that saw cultural landscapes in Britain forever transformed.

One of the most visible aspects of this transformation was the introduction and eventual mainstream acceptance of Caribbean cuisine. West Indian restaurants and food stalls, once rare sights, became staples in many British towns and cities, serving as both a taste of home for the diaspora and an invitation to Britons to partake in the culinary delights of the Caribbean.

Music and dance, too, underwent a renaissance of sorts as genres like reggae, ska, and calypso found eager audiences in Britain. These rhythms, born out of a complex history of struggle and celebration in the Caribbean, resonated with many and became symbols of multicultural Britain. The Notting Hill Carnival stands today as a testament to this fusion, a festival that started as an act of defiance against racial tensions and has grown to become one of the world's largest street festivals.

Yet, cultural fusion was not without its challenges. Resistance from native Britons, rooted in unfamiliarity and prejudice, often meant that the celebration of West Indian culture was met with hostility. This resistance, however, did not deter the Windrush generation nor their descendants. It galvanized them, fostering a sense of unity and pride within the community that enabled them to push for greater acceptance and recognition.

The profound impact of West Indian culture on Britain can also be traced through literature and the arts, where authors and artists of Caribbean descent have garnered critical acclaim and shaped the literary and visual narrative of modern Britain. From the poetic works of Derek Walcott to the dynamic canvases of Frank Bowling, the contributions of West Indian creatives have enriched Britain's cultural tapestry, illustrating the depth and diversity of their heritage.

The resistance and eventual cultural fusion contributed significantly to conversations about race and identity in Britain, challenging societal norms and encouraging a reflection on what it means to be British in a multicultural society. These dialogues were often uncomfortable but necessary, paving the way for legislative changes and the gradual dismantling of institutional barriers.

In education, West Indian parents and community leaders played pivotal roles in advocating for inclusivity and the acknowledgment of their history within the curriculum. Their efforts have led to a broader understanding and appreciation of the complexities of British history, highlighting the interconnectedness of the empire's past with present day multiculturalism.

The legacy of cultural fusion and resistance is not confined to past achievements. Today, it continues to inspire new generations who navigate their identity in a landscape that is, at once, both more accepting and yet reflective of historical prejudices. The story of the Windrush generation serves as a beacon, illustrating the power of culture, resilience, and the enduring quest for equality.

The spirit of the Windrush generation, encapsulated in their journey of cultural fusion and resistance, stands as a shining example of how communities can influence societal change beyond the confines of their original homeland. Their legacy, characterized by the blend of persistence, creativity, and unity, is a compelling narrative of how cultural diversity enriches societies.

This tale of cultural interweaving is not just a chapter in the history of the British Isles but a vibrant thread in the global tapestry of migration and integration. It is a poignant reminder that the forces of cultural fusion and resistance are not only transformative but are the heartbeats of progress.

As we reflect on the significance of the Windrush contribution, it becomes clear that their journey—marked by moments of hardship and triumph—has laid down a roadmap for future generations. It teaches us that cultural preservation and innovation, coupled with the courage to confront and navigate resistance, are the keystones to building a prosperous, inclusive future.

In the end, the story of the West Indian diaspora is not just one of assimilation but of profound resilience and contribution. It heralds the message that while the journey towards acceptance and prosperity may be fraught with obstacles, the persistent spirit of unity and the richness of one's cultural heritage are powerful catalysts for change.

The chapters that follow will delve deeper into the myriad ways the Windrush generation and their descendants have shaped, and continue to influence, the cultural, economic, and social landscapes of Britain and beyond. Their legacy is a testament to the enduring strength of diversity and the indomitable spirit of the human will to seek out a better life, not just for oneself but for future generations.

Chapter 3:
Defining Generational Wealth

In traversing the expansive and often rugged terrain of history, one encounters various definitions of wealth that span across cultures and epochs. However, the concept of generational wealth, particularly within the context of the Windrush generation, encompasses more than just the accumulation of financial assets. It's a tapestry woven from the resilience, aspirations, and accomplishments of those who ventured from the Caribbean to Britain, carrying with them dreams not just for their own prosperity, but for the thriving of future generations. Generational wealth, as we explore in this chapter, transcends the traditional confines of monetary riches to include the legacy of education, cultural identity, and the establishment of social and economic pillars that support the collective upliftment of a community. This holistic approach to wealth, which amalgamates both innovative avenues and time-honored strategies, not only enriches the current generation but also lays a robust foundation for the ones to come. In defining generational wealth, our aim is not merely to chart its tangible components but to inspire a deeper comprehension of its pivotal role in seeding a future where prosperity and well-being are within the reach of every descendant of the Windrush voyagers.

The Concept and Its Importance

Generational wealth, often termed as legacy wealth, extends beyond the mere accumulation of financial assets. It embodies the transmission of prosperity, knowledge, values, and opportunities from one generation to the next. This wealth isn't solely measured in currency, but in the rich tapestry of culture, education, real estate, businesses, and financial investments that are passed down, serving as both a foundation and a launching pad for successive generations.

In illuminating the essence of generational wealth, it's imperative to acknowledge its transformative power. The ability to bestow upon one's progeny not just the means to survive but to thrive, to pursue dreams unfettered by the constraints of financial hardship, is profound. It is a concept woven with the threads of hope, resilience, and foresight, traits emblematic of the Windrush generation whose legacy is a testament to the power of enduring optimism and strategic planning.

The importance of generational wealth cannot be overstated. It is a bulwark against the cycles of poverty that can ensnare families for generations. With financial security, each generation gains the freedom to explore education, entrepreneurial ventures, and investments that yield long-term benefits. Moreover, the psychological impact of knowing there is a financial safety net is liberating, fostering environments where creativity and innovation can flourish.

For the Windrush generation, creating generational wealth was more than a personal goal; it was a communal imperative. Facing systemic barriers and racial prejudice, establishing a financial foothold was a means of asserting dignity, ensuring stability, and laying a foundation for the generations that would follow. Their efforts were seeds planted in fertile ground, nurturing future successes that would extend far beyond their individual contributions.

Generational wealth also underscores the significance of legacy. In the context of the Windrush generation, legacy is not solely defined by what was left behind but also by what was built, struggled for, and ultimately achieved. It's about the intangible assets - the stories, wisdom, traditions, and values that imbue heirs with a sense of identity, belonging, and responsibility to their ancestors' sacrifices.

The journey towards generational wealth often begins with education. The profound emphasis on learning and intellectual growth cannot be overlooked. It is through education that generations have been empowered to break barriers, innovate, and forge paths towards financial independence. This legacy of prioritizing education has ripple effects, enriching communities and fueling socioeconomic growth.

Ownership plays a critical role in the creation of generational wealth. Ownership of land, property, and businesses not only provides a tangible asset to pass down but also instills a sense of pride and autonomy. It's a statement of belonging and permanence in a world that often made the Windrush generation feel transient and unwelcome.

Moreover, the proactive approach to financial planning and investment among the Caribbean diaspora has been pivotal. Despite the hurdles, they've navigated financial systems to save, invest, and acquire assets that appreciate over time. It's a narrative of resilience and savvy that has granted financial liberation to many.

The concept of generational wealth is also deeply rooted in the practice of community upliftment. The Windrush generation understood that their individual successes had ripple effects, benefiting extended families and communities. From pooling resources to assist one another in buying homes to investing in community businesses and educational funds, their model of cooperative economics has left an indelible mark on the landscapes of wealth creation.

Furthermore, the preservation and transmission of cultural heritage have been integral to the concept of generational wealth. Beyond financial assets, cultural practices, values, and traditions are priceless legacies that enrich the lives of descendants and provide a unique sense of identity and belonging. The Windrush generation's efforts to maintain their cultural roots while navigating a new homeland have ensured the vibrancy of their heritage for future generations.

Challenges to building and sustaining generational wealth certainly exist. From systemic barriers to economic volatility, the path is fraught with obstacles. Yet, the story of the Windrush generation illustrates that with determination, community support, and strategic planning, these challenges can be overcome. Their legacy is a beacon for future generations, illuminating a path towards prosperity and fulfillment.

As we delve deeper into the significance of generational wealth, it's critical to recognize its multifaceted nature. It's not just about accumulating wealth but about fostering environments where each generation can surpass the last in well-being, achievement, and impact. This holistic approach to wealth ensures that the legacy of the Windrush generation and their descendants will continue to flourish.

In conclusion, the concept of generational wealth and its importance cannot be understated. It's a powerful testament to the enduring spirit of the Windrush generation. Their legacy of perseverance, innovation, and community upliftment has laid a solid foundation for future generations. As we continue to explore the paths they've paved, their journey offers invaluable lessons in resilience, unity, and the transformative power of legacy wealth. Through understanding and embracing these principles, we can all aspire to build a future marked by prosperity, inclusion, and fulfillment.

In this light, the concept of generational wealth is not only a tribute to past accomplishments but also a guiding star for future endeavors. It invites us to imagine a world where wealth in all its forms - financial, cultural, educational - is not just preserved but expanded, ensuring that the legacies we leave behind are as enduring as they are enriching.

Traditional vs. Innovative Approaches

As we delve into the realm of generational wealth, it's essential to juxtapose the traditional approaches against the innovative strategies that have emerged over time. The conventional methods of building and preserving wealth have predominantly revolved around savings, investments in stocks, bonds, real estate, and the transference of these assets through inheritances. While these strategies have proven effective for many, the evolving global economy and technological advancements have ushered in a renewed perspective on wealth creation and distribution.

The concept of generational wealth is not merely about the accumulation of assets but also encompasses the imparting of values, knowledge, and opportunities across generations. This holistic approach challenges the traditional view and embraces innovative methods that align with the dynamic nature of today's world. The Windrush generation, amidst all adversities, has demonstrated a remarkable ability to adapt and innovate, laying down a blueprint for future generations to follow.

One of the key distinctions between traditional and innovative approaches lies in the emphasis on education and empowerment. Historically, education was often viewed as a means to secure a stable job and income. However, the Windrush saga teaches us the power of education as a tool for innovation, creative expression, and entrepreneurial ventures. This shift in perspective has profound implications for generational wealth, as it broadens the avenues through which wealth can be created and sustained.

Moreover, the innovative approaches to generational wealth recognize the value of cultural and artistic contributions. For the Windrush generation, art, music, and literature were not only sources of solace but also means of economic empowerment and legacy building. By leveraging their cultural capital, they carved out new spaces in British society, influencing not just the economy but also the socio-cultural landscape. This intersection of culture and commerce illustrates the expansive potential of innovative approaches to wealth generation.

Technology also plays a pivotal role in defining innovative strategies for building generational wealth. The digital revolution has democratized access to information, education, and financial markets, breaking down barriers that once made wealth creation a preserve for the few. The younger generations, riding on the legacy of their Windrush forebearers, are seizing these technological tools to craft novel pathways to wealth creation that transcend geographical and socioeconomic boundaries.

Entrepreneurship, particularly within the digital realm, emerges as a potent vehicle for generational wealth in the innovative approach. Unlike traditional business models, digital enterprises can start with minimal capital, harness the global market, and scale rapidly. This entrepreneurial spirit, inspired by the Windrush generation's resilience and resourcefulness, encourages a proactive stance towards wealth creation, where risks are embraced, and innovation is the guiding principle.

Moreover, the innovative approach advocates for financial literacy and wealth education from an early age. Understanding the intricacies of personal finance, investments, and wealth management empowers individuals to make informed decisions, avoid debt traps, and build sustainable wealth. This proactive education model is a departure from the traditional passive inheritance of wealth, ensuring that future generations not only inherit wealth but also the wisdom to grow it.

Collaborations and community networks form another cornerstone of innovative approaches to generational wealth. The Windrush generation's success was not just in individual achievements but also in their ability to mobilize community resources, share knowledge, and support one another. In today's globalized world, these networks extend beyond physical communities to virtual platforms, enabling diaspora communities to connect, collaborate, and co-create wealth across borders.

Furthermore, the focus on sustainable and socially responsible investing marks a critical aspect of innovative wealth-building strategies. Today's generations are increasingly aware of the environmental, social, and governance (ESG) aspects of investing. By aligning their investments with their values, they not only aim for financial returns but also contribute to positive social and environmental outcomes, ensuring that their wealth legacy is both prosperous and purposeful.

Embracing diversity and inclusivity is also integral to innovative approaches. The Windrush generation's journey underscored the challenges of exclusion and the strength found in diversity. Today, creating wealth opportunities that are inclusive and accessible to people from diverse backgrounds is seen as not just morally right but economically smart. This inclusive mindset catalyzes innovation, unlocks potential, and paves the way for a more equitable distribution of wealth.

At the heart of the innovative approach is the understanding that wealth is not a static asset to be preserved but a dynamic resource that can grow, evolve, and adapt to changing circumstances. This reflects a fundamental shift in mindset from scarcity to abundance, from preservation to creation. The lessons from the Windrush generation imbue us with the belief that no obstacle is insurmountable and that our collective spirit of resilience and innovation can forge paths to prosperity.

As we stand at the crossroads of tradition and innovation, it becomes evident that the journey of generational wealth is an ongoing narrative, shaped by our values, decisions, and actions. The legacy of the Windrush generation offers a testament to the power of innovation in the face of adversity. It serves as a beacon, guiding us towards a future where generational wealth is not just about the assets we accumulate but the legacy of empowerment, creativity, and resilience we leave behind.

In essence, bridging the divide between traditional and innovative approaches requires a harmonious blend of values, visionary thinking, and adaptability. It invites us to reimagine the possibilities of generational wealth, not as an end in itself but as a means to nurture, empower, and uplift future generations. As we embark on this journey, let us draw inspiration from the Windrush saga, ensuring that our endeavors in building generational wealth are as much about enriching our lives as they are about securing a prosperous future for the generations to come.

In conclusion, the journey of generational wealth, influenced by the Windrush legacy, underscores the importance of embracing both traditional and innovative approaches. By marrying the wisdom of the past with the possibilities of the future, we can chart a course towards a legacy of wealth that transcends financial prosperity and embodies the true essence of generational empowerment and fulfillment.

Chapter 4:
The Spirit of Innovation Among the Windrush Generation

In the wake of the chapters that lay the foundation of the Windrush saga, Chapter 4 stands as a testament to the undying spirit of innovation that the Windrush generation harbored within them. Upon setting foot on British soil, these pioneers were met not only with the challenge of integrating into a society that was vastly different from what they had known but also the necessity to carve out spaces for themselves where they could thrive. The adversity they faced did not deter them; instead, it fueled a burning desire to innovate, to turn the tides in their favor in a land that was both foreign and unwelcoming. They undertook roles that were pivotal in post-war Britain's recovery, yet went beyond mere labor contributions. These industrious souls laid the groundwork for a culture of entrepreneurship and creativity that would transcend generations. Their legacy, marked by an audacious willingness to venture into uncharted territories—be it in business, the arts, or social activism—has left an indelible mark on the fabric of British society and continues to inspire current and future generations. This chapter delves into the heart of their journey from mere survival to prosperity, shedding light on the innovative strategies they employed and the pioneering spirit that guided them. Through resilience and ingenuity, the Windrush generation not only navigated through the challenges of their time but also sowed the seeds of a prosperous future for those who would follow in their footsteps.

Case Studies of Innovation

In the tapestry of history, the spirit of innovation often emerges from the interstices of struggle and resilience. This has been vividly exemplified by the Windrush generation, whose arrival in Britain marked the beginning of a profound transformation not only within their own communities but also in the socio-economic landscape of Britain. Through a series of case studies, we explore how this generation leveraged innovation as both a survival mechanism and a pathway to prosperity.

One compelling narrative is that of Claudia Jones, a Trinidad-born journalist and activist, who utilized the power of the press to give a voice to the Caribbean community in Britain. Founding the influential newspaper, *West Indian Gazette*, Jones transcended traditional boundaries of advocacy by using journalism as a tool for social change. Her pioneering work culminated in the creation of the Notting Hill Carnival, an event that not only became a profound expression of Caribbean culture but also a testament to the innovative spirit of the Windrush generation.

Similarly, the entrepreneurial journey of Sam King stands as a beacon of innovation. King, a Windrush passenger, went on to co-found the *Caribbean Times* newspaper and became the first Black mayor of Southwark. His career encapsulated the ethos of turning challenges into stepping stones, as he navigated the complexities of British society to establish platforms that amplified the voices of his community.

Another domain where innovation was remarkably manifested is in the realm of cuisine. The Windrush generation introduced Britain to a plethora of Caribbean culinary delights. Frank Crichlow's 'Mangrove Restaurant' in Notting Hill became more than a dining establishment; it was a cultural hub that played a significant role in community organizing and activism. Through these culinary ventures, the Windrush migrants not only shared a taste of their homeland but also fostered a sense of community and belonging in a foreign land.

In the field of entertainment, the Windrush generation played a pivotal role in shaping Britain's musical landscape. The Trojan Records, established by Jamaican Lee Gopthal, was instrumental in bringing reggae and ska music to the British mainstream. This record label not only provided a platform for Caribbean artists but also fostered cultural fusion, influencing the emergence of new music genres such as two-tone and reggae punk. The resilience and creative ingenuity of these pioneers illustrated how the arts can serve as a powerful medium for cultural integration and innovation.

Educationally, figures like Bernard Coard, an educator from Grenada, used his expertise to innovate within the realm of education. Coard authored the seminal work, "How the West Indian Child is Made Educationally Subnormal in the British School System", sparking a national conversation on educational reform and equity. His advocacy led to significant policy changes and highlighted how innovation can stem from a deep understanding of systemic challenges.

Moreover, the healthcare sector profoundly benefited from the innovative approaches of the Windrush generation. The establishment of community-based health clinics by Caribbean nurses, who faced discrimination in mainstream healthcare institutions, filled a critical gap in medical care. These clinics not only provided essential health services but also incorporated holistic practices and cultural sensitivities, laying the groundwork for future innovations in community health outreach.

In the realm of law and advocacy, the establishment of the Black Legal Action Centre by members of the Caribbean diaspora marked a significant milestone in providing legal support and representation to marginalized communities. This initiative demonstrated innovation in social justice, reflecting a strategic approach to dismantling systemic barriers through legal avenues.

The case studies elucidated herein underscore the multifaceted dimensions of innovation that the Windrush generation brought to Britain. From media to cuisine, and music to healthcare, their legacy of innovation is a testament to their resilience, creativity, and unwavering commitment to community upliftment. As we delve deeper into their stories, it becomes evident that the spirit of innovation among the Windrush generation was not merely about survival; it was a bold declaration of their right to thrive, contribute, and fundamentally transform their new homeland.

In essence, the narrative of the Windrush generation is a profound reminder that innovation often flourishes most significantly in the face of adversity. Their legacy not only reshaped aspects of British culture and society but also offered invaluable lessons on the transformative power of innovative thinking and action. As we look to the future, the pioneering spirit of the Windrush generation serves as an enduring source of inspiration, urging us to approach challenges with creativity, resilience, and a steadfast commitment to progress and equity.

Indeed, the case studies of innovation among the Windrush generation are not just historical accounts; they are beacon lights for future generations. They exemplify how vision, tenacity, and ingenuity can transcend barriers, catalyze change, and create lasting legacies. As we continue to navigate the complexities of the modern world, the stories of these trailblazers remind us that innovation is not merely a tool for economic advancement but a pathway to creating more inclusive and vibrant communities.

From Survival to Prosperity As we delve deeper into the narrative of the Windrush generation, it's crucial to acknowledge the journey from mere survival to the attainment of prosperity. This transition wasn't merely a matter of economic success but also a significant cultural and psychological shift for the West Indian community in Britain. The initial years were fraught with challenges, including racial prejudice, social isolation, and economic hardship. Yet, the unwavering spirit and resilience of this generation laid the groundwork for a legacy of prosperity and success that would benefit future generations.

The concept of generational wealth, which we explore in depth in Chapter 3, was not something the Windrush pioneers could have imagined in their early days in Britain. However, their innate desire for a better life and determination to overcome obstacles set the stage for what would eventually evolve into endeavors aimed at securing financial stability and prosperity for themselves and their descendants.

One of the most striking aspects of the Windrush generation's journey to prosperity was their innovative approach to navigating a new social and economic landscape. As we see in Chapter 4, their spirit of innovation was crucial. Confronted with a labor market that was often hostile and discriminatory, many individuals from this generation carved out niches for themselves in various sectors, displaying remarkable adaptability and entrepreneurial spirit.

Their ventures ranged from setting up small businesses that catered to the needs of the West Indian community, such as grocery stores, barber shops, and music venues, to entering professions where they could utilize their skills and talents to the fullest. This entrepreneurial spirit was not just a means to economic independence but also served as a beacon of inspiration for future generations, illustrating the power of resilience and hard work.

Moreover, the cultural contributions of the Windrush generation played a pivotal role in their journey from survival to prosperity. As highlighted in Chapter 5, their artistic and cultural innovations, particularly in music and literature, not only enriched the cultural tapestry of Britain but also provided them with platforms to express their identities, share their stories, and connect with wider audiences. This cultural ascendancy was instrumental in elevating their social standing and fostering a sense of community and belonging.

In the realm of economics, as discussed in Chapter 6, the entrepreneurial ventures of the Windrush generation laid the foundation for a burgeoning West Indian business community in Britain. These businesses not only contributed to the British economy but also facilitated the circulation of wealth within the West Indian community, thereby playing a crucial role in the creation of generational wealth.

The integration of technology and education, themes explored in Chapters 7 and 8, further accelerated the transition from survival to prosperity. Embracing technological advancements and prioritizing education empowered the Windrush descendants to navigate the complexities of the modern world, seize new opportunities, and continue the legacy of innovation and economic success established by their forebears.

As we reflect on the transformative journey of the Windrush generation, it becomes clear that their legacy is not merely one of survival against the odds but also a testament to the extraordinary potential for prosperity through resilience, innovation, and community. Their story serves as a powerful reminder of the indomitable spirit of individuals who, in the face of adversity, forge paths to a brighter future, not just for themselves but for generations to come.

In essence, the Windrush generation's transition from survival to prosperity encapsulates a broader narrative of human endurance, creativity, and the relentless pursuit of a better life. Their enduring legacy continues to inspire not only the West Indian community but also individuals and communities across the globe, highlighting the universal values of resilience, innovation, and the indomitable human spirit.

Thus, as we chart the course for future generations, let us draw from the wellspring of wisdom and inspiration left by the Windrush pioneers. Their journey from survival to prosperity underscores the profound impact that determination, innovation, and community solidarity can have on shaping a legacy of enduring success and fulfillment. It is a powerful testament to the fact that, even in the face of seemingly insurmountable challenges, it is possible to chart a path to prosperity that leaves a lasting legacy for future generations.

Pioneering in Unfamiliar Territories

The chapter at hand delves into the audacious journey of the Windrush generation as they navigated and conquered uncharted realms. This era marks an extraordinary chapter where courage, vision, and relentless innovation fused, charting a course towards unprecedented achievements. Their legacy, imbued with a spirit of exploration, stands as a testament to their indomitable resolve.

In the wake of their arrival, the Windrush pioneers found themselves ensconced in a milieu utterly alien from the Caribbean shores they had left behind. The stark contrast of the British landscape, coupled with the frigid climate, was but the first of many unfamiliar territories they would navigate. Yet, it was in these unaccustomed surroundings that their innovative spirits thrived, driven by necessity and an unwavering desire to prosper.

The employment landscape post-World War II presented both challenges and opportunities. Many of the Windrush generation seized upon sectors that were crying out for manpower, such as the National Health Service, public transport, and construction. The shortage of labor in these areas paved the way for their initial entry into the British economy, but it was their spirit of innovation that allowed them to ascend beyond the confines of menial labor.

Confronted with limited advancement opportunities and rampant discrimination, they began to carve out their niches. From the culinary businesses that introduced Caribbean flavor to the British palette, to the burgeoning music scene which saw the rise of Calypso and later reggae in the UK, their contributions were both diverse and profound. Each endeavor was a pioneering step, a foray into unfamiliar territory with determination at its helm.

Beyond entrepreneurship, they ventured into the arts and culture, embedding their rich heritage into the fabric of British society. This not only provided a semblance of home but also educated and enriched the cultural landscape of their new nation. Their pioneering efforts in these arenas laid the groundwork for future generations, demonstrating the power of cultural exchange and innovation.

However, it's important to note that these pioneering endeavors were not without their hurdles. Navigating a system that was often set against them required not only innovation but sheer resilience. The institutional barriers erected by a society grappling with its own post-colonial identity meant that each success was hard-fought.

Moreover, the Windrush generation's legacy of pioneering extends into the realm of social and political activism. They were instrumental in laying the foundations for the civil rights movements in the UK, challenging racial inequalities and fighting for justice. Their tireless efforts paved the way for the enactment of anti-discrimination laws, marking significant progress in the battle for equality.

Their trailblazing path also illuminated the importance of education as a tool for empowerment and upward mobility. Recognizing the limitations of their own access to formal education, many within the Windrush generation placed a heightened emphasis on ensuring their children and subsequent generations could benefit from the educational opportunities they lacked. This push towards academia was yet another terrain they pioneered, contributing significantly to the shaping of future leaders, academics, and professionals.

In reflecting on these pioneering achievements, it becomes evident that the Windrush generation's journey was marked by a relentless pursuit of innovation driven by necessity, vision, and an unwavering commitment to progress. Their ability to adapt, overcome, and eventually thrive is a powerful narrative that continues to inspire.

As we delve deeper into their stories, we uncover an enduring legacy of resilience and innovation. The Windrush generation's experience is a beacon, illuminating the path for those who find themselves navigating unfamiliar territories. It serves as a reminder that foresight, tenacity, and a pioneering spirit can overcome the most daunting of challenges.

Their contributions to the economic, cultural, and social landscapes of their adopted homeland are a testament to the transformative power of innovation. It is through their pioneering efforts that they were able to establish a foundation not only for their prosperity but also for the enrichment of a society that was, at first, resistant to their presence.

However, the journey of the Windrush pioneers also underscores the importance of community and collective action. In facing the trials and tribulations of integration, they drew strength from their cultural bonds, leaning on one another to forge ahead. This sense of unity and shared purpose was pivotal in their successful navigation of unfamiliar territories.

Today, as we witness new generations grappling with their own challenges, the pioneering spirit of the Windrush generation offers invaluable lessons. It speaks to the power of resilience, the importance of innovation, and the unyielding pursuit of progress. In a world that continues to evolve at a rapid pace, these principles remain as relevant as ever.

In conclusion, the Windrush generation's narrative of pioneering in unfamiliar territories is a profound legacy that transcends time. It is a story of hope, resilience, and indefatigable spirit that serves as a guiding light for future generations. As we chart our own courses through unexplored realms, let us draw inspiration from their journey, embracing the spirit of innovation to navigate and conquer the challenges that lie ahead.

Through this exploration of the Windrush generation's pioneering endeavors, we are reminded of the unbreakable human spirit's capacity to innovate, adapt, and thrive. Their legacy is not just a chapter in history but a continuous source of inspiration, urging us all to forge ahead with courage, determination, and a pioneering mindset that can transform the unfamiliar into the extraordinary.

Chapter 5:
Creativity in the Midst of Adversity

The journey of the Windrush generation is a testament to the resilience of the human spirit, a theme that finds profound expression in Chapter 5, "Creativity in the Midst of Adversity." As these individuals navigated the challenges of displacement and integration into an often unwelcoming society, they turned to creativity as a means of survival and self-expression. This chapter delves into the artistic and cultural innovations that not only provided an outlet for the Windrush generation but also left an indelible mark on the world. The evolution of Calypso from a form of news communication on the islands to a staple on the British music scene exemplifies how adversity was transformed into opportunity. The journey from the Caribbean colonies to global stages underscored the universal power of creativity to transcend boundaries and foster connection. Through a detailed exploration of these topics, "Creativity in the Midst of Adversity" aims to inspire readers by showing how the Windrush generation leveraged their artistic talents to forge pathways to recognition, influence, and generational prosperity, thereby casting a long legacy that continues to influence and inspire future generations.

Artistic and Cultural Innovations

In a world where adversity is often the catalyst for creativity, the aftermath of the Windrush era serves as a profound testament to the resilience and innovative spirit of Caribbean migrants and their descendants. This section delves into the riveting journey of artistic and cultural innovations birthed from the struggles and triumphs of a generation seeking to carve out a space for themselves in a foreign land. It is a narrative that intertwines the persistence of cultural identity with the transformative power of creativity.

The allure of the Caribbean's rich artistic traditions, when transplanted onto British soil, underwent a fascinating metamorphosis. The migrants brought with them not just their hopes and dreams, but a treasure trove of cultural expressions ripe for exploration and reinterpretation in their new environment. These included diverse forms of music, art, literature, and fashion, each carrying the indelible mark of a civilization shaped by history, geography, and the confluence of various cultural influences over centuries.

Music, in particular, emerged as a significant medium through which the Windrush generation articulated their experiences, aspirations, and challenges. The rhythm of calypso, originating from the French and African influences of Trinidad and Tobago, found a new audience in Britain, morphing into what would later be celebrated as a quintessential form of British-Caribbean expression. Lyrics that spoke of longing, diasporic life, and social commentary resonated with both Caribbean migrants and the wider British population, fostering a sense of community and understanding.

Similarly, the visual arts scene experienced a vibrant surge of creativity as artists of Caribbean descent began to gain recognition. Their canvases became the sites of cultural dialogues, merging Caribbean aesthetics with European techniques and themes. This fusion not only challenged traditional norms within the British art world but also provided a platform for the exploration of identity, belonging, and the multi-layered narratives of migration.

Literature and poetry flourished, with writers such as Sam Selvon and John Agard weaving tales and verses that captured the complexity of Windrush experiences. Their works, characterized by a blend of humor, satire, and poignant reflections, shed light on the lives of immigrants navigating a society marked by both opportunity and prejudice. Through their storytelling, these authors carved out spaces for Caribbean voices within the British literary canon, contributing to the broader dialogue on race, culture, and identity.

Fashion, too, became a significant avenue for cultural expression and innovation. Migrants infused their styles with a blend of Caribbean vibrancy and British practicality, creating distinctive looks that would influence the fashion industry for decades to come. This was not merely a matter of aesthetics but a bold statement of identity and independence, a reclaiming of space in a society that was often less than welcoming.

The influence of Caribbean culture extended well into the realms of the culinary arts. Caribbean cuisine, with its unique blend of flavors, spices, and cooking techniques, began to make its mark on the British food scene. From street food stalls to acclaimed restaurants, the culinary traditions of the Caribbean offered both comfort to those longing for a taste of home and a delightful encounter with the unfamiliar for the British palate.

Amidst this vibrant cultural renaissance, the role of community organizations became pivotal. These institutions served not only as gathering spots but also as incubators for cultural preservation and innovation. They provided platforms for emerging artists, musicians, poets, and culinary adventurers to showcase their talents, exchange ideas, and collaborate on projects that would carry their cultural heritage into new realms of expression.

Moreover, the practices of cultural education and mentorship emerged as crucial components of this landscape. Seasoned artists, musicians, and writers took it upon themselves to nurture the talents of younger generations, ensuring the transmission of knowledge, techniques, and traditions. This mentorship cultivated a sense of continuity and evolution within the artistic and cultural practices of the Caribbean diaspora, laying the groundwork for future innovation.

The impact of these cultural innovations was profound, extending far beyond the confines of the Caribbean community. They contributed to a reshaping of Britain's cultural landscape, fostering a greater appreciation for diversity and inclusivity. The ripples of these innovations traveled globally, influencing artistic and cultural movements worldwide and testament to the far-reaching impact of the Windrush generation's creativity. It is a clear illustration of how adversity, when met with resilience and ingenuity, can yield a legacy of richness and diversity that enriches societies for generations to come.

As we reflect on the artistic and cultural innovations sparked by the Windrush generation, it is essential to recognize the broader implications for understanding the dynamics of migration, integration, and cultural exchange. These narratives underscore the vital role of creativity as a mechanism for navigating and transcending the challenges of displacement, illustrating the potential for adversity to be transformed into a source of strength, connection, and communal identity.

The legacy of the Windrush generation's artistic and cultural contributions continues to inspire and inform current and future generations. It serves as a reminder that the essence of creativity lies in its ability to break boundaries, forge connections, and illuminate the shared humanity that binds us all. In the pursuit of generational wealth and wellbeing, the lessons of resilience, innovation, and unity embedded in this legacy offer invaluable guidance and hope for the road ahead.

Indeed, the story of artistic and cultural innovations in the midst of adversity is not just a chapter in the history of the Windrush generation but a beacon that lights the way for all who seek to turn challenges into opportunities for growth and expression. It is a testament to the enduring power of creativity to not only survive but thrive, shaping a more vibrant, inclusive, and prosperous world for generations to come.

The Calypso Legacy As we delve into the artistic and cultural innovations birthed from the adversities faced by the Windrush generation, a significant chapter of this story revolves around the enduring legacy of Calypso music. This music genre, originating from the Caribbean, particularly Trinidad and Tobago, played a pivotal role in not only providing solace to the newly arrived West Indians in post-war Britain but also in asserting their cultural identity amidst a backdrop of racial and social challenges.

Calypso's migration to British shores in the late 1940s and early 1950s, carried by the Windrush pioneers, served as a beacon of the Caribbean spirit. It was, for many, a nostalgic reminder of home but also acted as a medium to voice social and political critiques, cleverly wrapped in its rhythmic and melodic prowess. The music thus became both a source of comfort and a tool for activism.

The impact of Calypso in Britain was profound. In an era where racial segregation and discrimination were rampant, Calypso clubs and nights provided spaces where West Indians could freely express themselves, celebrate their heritage, and find a sense of belonging. These gatherings were not exclusive; they welcomed anyone who appreciated the sounds and stories encapsulated in Calypso music, thus fostering multi-cultural interactions and understanding.

Calypso's legacy is not only limited to its contribution to Britain's musical landscape but extends into its influence on subsequent generations. It paved the way for the acceptance and popularity of other Caribbean music genres such as Reggae and Soca, further enriching the British cultural tapestry. Additionally, Calypso's storytelling tradition has lived on, inspiring contemporary musicians and artists in narrating their experiences and reflections on society.

The resilience of the Windrush generation, mirrored in the perseverance and evolution of Calypso music, offers invaluable lessons in creativity and innovation in the face of adversity. Calypso became a channel through which the community could articulate its hopes, fears, and dreams, thus transforming their struggles into an empowering narrative that has left a lasting mark on the world.

This legacy of transformation and triumph is a testament to the indomitable spirit of the Windrush settlers. It serves as a reminder that culture and arts are powerful tools for change and advocacy. The Calypso saga encourages future generations to harness their heritage and creativity as vehicles for expressing identity, challenging injustices, and forging unity.

The story of Calypso within the Windrush narrative is a vibrant illustration of how art can serve as a lighthouse in turbulent times, guiding communities towards mutual understanding and respect. It underscores the importance of preserving cultural expressions as integral to the socio-cultural fabric of societies, bridging gaps between diverse groups and generations.

In light of the Calypso legacy, it becomes evident that achieving prosperity and fulfillment extends beyond financial wealth. It encompasses the richness of one's cultural inheritance and the ability to inspire change and foster community through artistic expression. The journey of Calypso music from the Caribbean to the streets of London epitomizes the broader journey of the Windrush generation—a trek from hardship to hope, from invisibility to indelible influence.

As we continue to unravel the multifaceted legacy of the Windrush generation, the story of Calypso stands out as a beacon of resilience, innovation, and unity. It exemplifies how cultural heritage can be leveraged to create a lasting impact, enabling future generations to navigate the complexities of identity, diversity, and belonging in a globalized world.

The Calypso legacy, with its rich melodies, poignant narratives, and vibrant rhythms, remains a powerful emblem of the enduring strength and creativity of the Caribbean diaspora. It challenges us to reflect on the ways in which we can embrace our diverse backgrounds to build a more inclusive and equitable society, making the Calypso legacy not just a chapter in history but a continuous source of inspiration and hope for the future.

From Caribbean Colonies to Global Stages

The journey from the Caribbean colonies to the global stages is not merely a tale of geographical movement. It is a saga of transformation, resilience, and triumph. The Caribbean, known for its stunning landscapes and rich cultural tapestry, has also been a crucible of creativity and innovation. This narrative begins in the aftermath of World War II, a period characterized by upheaval and the dawning realization that the future demanded change.

In the heart of adversity, the Windrush generation emerged as harbingers of that change. They crossed oceans not only in search of better lives but also brought with them the seeds of cultural dynamism that would eventually flourish on global stages. Music, literature, art, and culinary traditions from the Caribbean colonies began to intertwine with those of their new homes, creating rich, hybrid identities. The global journey was set in motion by those whose initial steps were taken on the decks of the Windrush.

Calypso and reggae, which sprang from the soul of the Caribbean, found their way onto the airwaves and stages of the world, speaking the language of freedom, resistance, and human dignity. Artists like Bob Marley didn't just share music; they shared the story of a people's struggle, making reggae an anthem for equality and justice worldwide. This music, born from the experience of colonial oppression, became a universal symbol of resilience and unity.

Literature too became a vessel for the Caribbean's voice. Authors such as Derek Walcott and V.S. Naipaul, who rooted their narratives in the Caribbean experience, achieved global recognition, including the Nobel Prize in Literature. Their stories transcended geographical boundaries, showcasing the complexity of post-colonial identity and the indomitable spirit of their people.

In the realm of visual arts, the vibrant palettes and evocative motifs of Caribbean painters such as Chris Ofili and

Jean-Michel Basquiat have captivated audiences worldwide. Their works, which often explore themes of heritage, identity, and the legacy of colonialism, have not only garnered international acclaim but have also sparked critical conversations about race, history, and politics on the global stage.

The culinary traditions of the Caribbean have also made their indelible mark globally. With a fusion of African, Indian, European, and indigenous influences, Caribbean cuisine embodies the essence of cultural blending. Chefs and restaurateurs of Caribbean heritage have been pivotal in introducing these rich flavors to the world, transforming global dining experiences by showcasing the diversity and depth of Caribbean culinary arts.

Moreover, the Caribbean diaspora has made significant contributions to the fields of science, technology, and business, demonstrating that the journey from Caribbean colonies to global stages is not confined to cultural expressions alone. Figures such as Shirley Jackson, a physicist who has significantly contributed to telecommunications technology, exemplify the diaspora's impact on global innovation.

This global odyssey has not been without its challenges. Racism, xenophobia, and socioeconomic hurdles have tested the resilience and determination of the Caribbean diaspora. Yet, these trials have only fueled their drive to excel and to assert their place on the world stage.

The influence of the Caribbean diaspora extends beyond their achievements. It lies also in their ability to inspire generations across the globe. Their journey underscores the message that heritage and identity are powerful tools for overcoming adversity and achieving greatness.

As we reflect on the journey from Caribbean colonies to global stages, it's evident that the legacy of the Windrush generation is not solely about what was left behind but, more importantly, about what was carried forward: hope, creativity, and an indomitable spirit. The paths they paved have opened doors for future generations to walk through, with the conviction that their contributions are valuable not only in their new homes but on the global platform.

This section of our narrative celebrates the spirit of innovation and resilience demonstrated by individuals of Caribbean descent. It is an homage to their journey and an acknowledgment of their profound impact on the world. It serves as an inspiration, offering invaluable lessons on the power of embracing one's heritage while contributing to the global tapestry of culture and innovation.

In essence, the story from Caribbean colonies to global stages is a testament to the fact that limitations and boundaries are surmountable. The Windrush generation and their descendants have shown that adversity can be a catalyst for creativity, innovation, and success on the world's stage. As we look forward, their legacy illuminates the path, encouraging future generations to pursue their aspirations with dignity, pride, and an unwavering belief in their potential to contribute to a richer, more diverse world.

Thus, as we delve into the chapters that follow, let us carry with us the lessons of resilience, innovation, and the importance of cultural heritage. The journey from the Caribbean colonies to the global stages is a powerful reminder that, regardless of where we come from, our dreams and our voices have the power to resonate across the world. Let this legacy inspire us to continue building bridges of understanding and to strive for a future where every individual has the opportunity to shine on the global stage.

Chapter 6:
Economic Fortunes:
The Entrepreneurial Spirit

In the heart of post-war Britain, a remarkable transformation was underway, fueled not just by the efforts to rebuild a nation, but by the indomitable spirit of the Windrush generation. This chapter delves into how, against a backdrop of adversity and systemic challenges, West Indian immigrants channeled their entrepreneurial spirit to create economic fortunes that have left an indelible mark on the British economy and beyond. The rise of West Indian businesses is not merely a testament to individual success but a beacon of hope for future generations. Embracing the dual forces of creativity and resilience, these trailblazers overcame hurdles to establish a wide array of businesses, from culinary ventures that brought the tantalizing flavors of the Caribbean to British streets, to fashion and music enterprises that played pivotal roles in the cultural amalgamation of Britain. Through their journeys, we witness the power of entrepreneurship not just as a means for economic survival, but as a profound vehicle for community building, cultural preservation, and the forging of generational wealth. As they navigated the maze of challenges, their triumphs echoed the unyielding belief that within each obstacle lies an opportunity waiting to be seized. Their stories, rich with lessons of perseverance, innovation, and strategic foresight, offer invaluable motivation for anyone aspiring to carve out pathways to prosperity and fulfillment, underscoring the undeniable impact of the entrepreneurial spirit in charting economic fortunes.

The Rise of West Indian Businesses

The genesis of West Indian businesses in post-war Britain is a tale interwoven with resilience, innovation, and a relentless drive towards economic empowerment. The Windrush generation, despite facing formidable social and economic barriers, laid down the foundational stones for a legacy of entrepreneurial success. This narrative explores the multifaceted journey of West Indian migrants who, against the backdrop of adversity, cultivated prosperity not only for themselves but also for future generations.

In the immediate aftermath of World War II, the British economy was in a state of disarray, requiring significant labor to rebuild what had been lost or destroyed. West Indian migrants stepped into this breach, initially seeking employment in public services, manufacturing, and transport. However, they quickly identified gaps in the market, especially in providing products and services to cater to the needs and tastes of the West Indian community, thus marking the embryonic stage of West Indian enterprise in Britain.

One of the first and most iconic businesses to emerge was the West Indian barber shop. These establishments were more than just places to get a haircut; they became cultural hubs where expatriates could connect, share news from home, and discuss their experiences in a new land. The barber shop was emblematic of how West Indian businesses managed to fuse economic activity with community building.

Following closely was the rise of Caribbean eateries and grocery stores. These businesses not only catered to the culinary tastes of the West Indian diaspora but also introduced British society to an explosion of Caribbean flavors, paving the way for what would eventually become a love affair between Britain and foods like jerk chicken, curry goat, and roti. What started as small, family-run ventures blossomed into cornerstone institutions in their communities.

Record shops and music venues also played a pivotal role in the business landscape, providing access to Caribbean music which was largely unavailable through mainstream outlets. These spaces were instrumental in popularizing genres such as reggae and ska amongst the wider British population, showcasing the intercultural exchange catalyzed by West Indian entrepreneurship.

The trajectory of West Indian businesses also points to an acute understanding of the economic principle of self-reliance. Denied opportunities and faced with discrimination in the wider job market, West Indian migrants channeled their entrepreneurial energies into creating opportunities for themselves and others in their community. By doing so, they not only generated wealth but also instilled a sense of ownership and pride within the diaspora.

The evolution of these businesses reflects a journey of adaptation and resilience. In many cases, what began as small, makeshift operations eventually grew into professionally managed establishments that catered to a wide range of customers. This transition was not without its challenges. Business owners grappled with issues such as access to financing, navigating bureaucratic regulations, and overcoming racial prejudice.

Yet, the success stories cannot be understated. By the 1980s and 1990s, many West Indian businesses had become integral parts of their local economies, contributing significantly to the multicultural tapestry of Britain. These accomplishments bear testament to the entrepreneurial acumen and hard work of the Windrush generation and their descendants.

The legacy of West Indian businesses goes beyond their economic impact. They have played a crucial role in fostering social cohesion, offering platforms for dialogue, and promoting a deeper understanding and appreciation of West Indian culture. The business ventures that flourished are vivid examples of how commerce can serve as a vehicle for cultural diplomacy.

Furthermore, these enterprises have provided invaluable mentorship and inspiration for younger generations within the diaspora. They stand as tangible proof of what can be achieved despite facing systemic barriers, inspiring a new wave of entrepreneurs who continue to build on the foundations laid by their predecessors.

It's important to recognize the symbiotic relationship between West Indian businesses and the wider British society. As these enterprises grew, they facilitated greater intercultural connections, challenged stereotypes, and contributed to the dynamic diversity that is now celebrated as a hallmark of British identity.

As we reflect on the journey of West Indian businesses, it's evident that their rise was not merely about economic gain. It was a movement rooted in community upliftment, cultural pride, and breaking new ground in a foreign land. The challenges they navigated and the triumphs they celebrated encapsulate the indomitable spirit of the Windrush generation.

In modern times, the entrepreneurial spirit that drove the establishment and growth of West Indian businesses remains a beacon of hope. It serves not only as a testament to what has been achieved but also as an inspiration for future ventures. The legacy of these businesses underscores the critical role of entrepreneurship in advancing generational wealth, well-being, and the ongoing quest for equity and inclusion.

As we look to the future, the story of West Indian businesses continues to be written by ambitious entrepreneurs who draw on the rich heritage of their forebears. These endeavors, grounded in resilience, creativity, and a deep sense of community, promise to further enrich the British economic and cultural landscape. The rise of West Indian businesses is a powerful reminder that within stories of struggle, there lie boundless opportunities for triumph and legacy building.

In conclusion, the narratives of West Indian businesses are a testament to the power of entrepreneurship as a conduit for change. They remind us that with determination, community support, and a clear vision, barriers can be transformed into bridges towards success. As we honor the contributions of the Windrush generation, we are inspired to continue forging paths of prosperity, armed with the lessons from those who have navigated the journey before us.

Challenges and Triumphs The entrepreneurial journey of the Windrush generation is a saga that exemplifies resilience, innovation, and the unyielding spirit to overcome. The West Indian businesses that took root in the heart of Britain's economic landscape faced a milieu fraught with societal, financial, and institutional challenges. Their stories, however, transcend these barriers, serving as a beacon of hope and a lesson in perseverance.

The inception of West Indian entrepreneurship in Britain was met with skepticism and outright discrimination. These pioneers navigated a market that was unaccustomed, and at times hostile, to their products and services. Access to capital — the lifeblood of any fledgling business — was severely constrained, as mainstream financial institutions often hesitated to back ventures spearheaded by the Windrush settlers. This financial ostracism necessitated a shift towards a more communal approach to funding, laying the groundwork for a resilient and self-sustaining business ecosystem within their communities.

Moreover, regulatory hurdles imposed additional barriers for these entrepreneurs. The labyrinthine nature of British business laws, coupled with a lack of familiarity and support, meant that many West Indian business owners had to learn through trial and error. Yet, it was this very challenge that instilled in them a pioneering spirit. They became adept at navigating these complexities, often transforming obstacles into opportunities to innovate and thrive.

The West Indian businesses, ranging from small eateries and music shops to barber shops and import-export enterprises, soon began to engrave their presence in the British economic fabric. They did not just cater to the Caribbean diaspora but also introduced the wider British population to a spectrum of Caribbean culture. This cultural exchange was pivotal, not only in fostering community bonds but also in gradually dispelling the mists of prejudice and misunderstanding.

The triumph of the Windrush entrepreneurs is not merely measured by their economic success but also by their profound impact on the British socio-cultural landscape. They laid the foundations for what would become a vibrant, multicultural Britain. Their successes challenged and slowly shifted perceptions, creating a space for future generations of immigrants to envision and build their dreams.

Equally inspiring are the stories of business ventures that became community hubs, offering support and guidance to new immigrants. These enterprises often extended beyond their commercial interests, becoming involved in social issues and advocating for the rights and welfare of the Windrush generation and their descendants. Their legacy is a rich tapestry of cultural integration, economic contribution, and social justice.

However, the journey of West Indian entrepreneurship in Britain is still an evolving narrative. Challenges persist, especially in an increasingly globalized economy that demands constant innovation and adaptation. Yet, the foundational principles of community support, innovative thinking, and relentless drive, anchored by the Windrush generation, continue to guide and inspire.

The impact of these entrepreneurial ventures transcends economic measures; they have played a seminal role in shaping a more inclusive and diverse British society. They remind us that the path to prosperity is often fraught with obstacles, but it is the courage to persevere, the wisdom to innovate, and the strength to stand united that heralds true triumph.

As we look to the future, the stories of the Windrush entrepreneurs serve as a potent reminder of the power of resilience and the enduring value of a community centered on mutual support and shared success. Their legacy is a beacon for future generations, illuminating a path not only to economic prosperity but to a richer, more inclusive society.

In conclusion, the entrepreneurial spirit of the Windrush generation is a testament to the enduring human capacity to overcome adversity through innovation, unity, and an unwavering belief in the potential for progress. Their triumphs against numerous challenges not only reshaped their own destinies but also left an indelible mark on the fabric of British society. They continue to inspire a new generation of entrepreneurs and community leaders, proving that from the greatest challenges can emerge the most enduring triumphs.

Chapter 7:
Bridging the Gap: Technology and Innovation

In the evolution of the Windrush legacy, the fusion of technology and innovation stands as a cornerstone for the diaspora's journey towards economic empowerment and generational wealth. The digital age has unfolded as a double-edged sword, presenting unparalleled challenges while simultaneously offering groundbreaking opportunities. For descendants of the Windrush generation, harnessing the power of technology has been instrumental in transcending traditional barriers to wealth creation. This era is marked by an impressive adaptability, with members of the Caribbean diaspora leveraging digital platforms to launch businesses, foster community connections, and create a fortified presence in the global market. The essence of this chapter underscores a pivotal shift from mere survival to thriving in a technologically driven landscape. It celebrates the resilience and ingenuity of a community that, despite the vicissitudes of time and geography, continues to innovate, inspire, and influence. Through an exploration of the digital revolution's impact, this segment not only delineates the pathways carved by the Windrush descendants in the realms of e-commerce, digital art, and virtual enterprises but also highlights how these advancements are leveraged to bridge the economic disparities faced by their forebearers. In essence, technology and innovation emerge not just as tools for wealth creation, but as beacons of hope, illuminating a future where prosperity and wellbeing are attainable legacies for subsequent generations.

The Digital Revolution and the Caribbean Diaspora

In an era where technology bridges continents and transforms societies, the Caribbean diaspora stands at the threshold of unprecedented change. The digital revolution, a term that encapsulates the shift from traditional industry to an economy based on digital technology, harbors both challenges and immense opportunities for those connected to the Caribbean.

The migration stories of the Windrush generation, while rich with tales of perseverance and cultural fusion, also highlight a relentless pursuit of prosperity and stability. Today, amidst the bytes and bits of the digital age, this pursuit continues, albeit on a radically different landscape.

For the Caribbean diaspora, technology has not only facilitated the preservation of cultural identities across oceans but has also opened doors to create and participate in global markets. From the vantage point of the digital economy, the skills, creativity, and entrepreneurial spirit of the Caribbean people are assets of untold value.

Online platforms have become the new marketplace, allowing Caribbean artisans, musicians, and entrepreneurs to showcase their work to a global audience without the barriers of geographical isolation. E-commerce, social media, and digital marketing have leveled the playing field, where interest and quality dictate market success rather than access to physical spaces in affluent locales.

Innovation within the diaspora doesn't stop at market access. The technology sector itself, with its infinite appetite for fresh ideas and diverse perspectives, offers fertile ground for Caribbean individuals adept in coding, digital design, and various IT specialties. Startups founded by members of the Caribbean diaspora are becoming more commonplace, not just in Silicon Valley but also in burgeoning tech hubs around the world.

However, with opportunity comes challenge. Access to technology remains uneven, both within the Caribbean and in diaspora communities abroad. Bridging this digital divide is crucial. Education and investment in digital literacy can empower more individuals to participate fully in the digital economy, turning potential into prosperity.

Moreover, the narrative of technology as a tool for economic advancement is only one part of the story. Social networks and communication technologies have played a significant role in connecting dispersed families and communities, allowing them to maintain a sense of belonging and cultural continuity. Virtual spaces host vibrant Caribbean festivals, book clubs, and forums, where discussions range from politics and societal issues to sharing recipes and musical talents.

This digital connectivity not only supports cultural preservation but also fosters a global network that can mobilize quickly in support of social justice causes, humanitarian efforts, and disaster relief, providing a new dimension to the concept of diaspora as a community without borders.

Furthermore, the digital revolution offers a unique opportunity for the Caribbean diaspora to engage with their heritage in innovative ways. Digital archives and virtual reality experiences bring historical narratives and ancestral knowledge to life, inspiring new generations to explore and embrace their heritage.

The transformative power of technology also extends to education, where online courses and resources break down barriers to learning, making it more accessible than ever. Through these digital platforms, individuals can acquire new skills, earn qualifications, and ultimately increase their economic mobility, ensuring that the legacy of the Windrush generation continues to evolve with the times.

Collaboration across the diaspora is key to harnessing the full potential of the digital revolution. Networking platforms specifically designed for Caribbean professionals facilitate mentorship, investment, and partnership opportunities, weaving a supportive fabric that can lift entire communities.

As we look to the future, it's evident that the digital revolution offers a pathway to not only preserve the rich legacy of the Caribbean diaspora but also to build upon it. Engaging with technology and innovation opens up a world of possibilities for creating generational wealth and wellbeing, aligning perfectly with the aspirations that have guided the Windrush descendants through the decades.

Yet, embracing the digital age requires vigilance. Evolving technologies such as artificial intelligence and big data analytics promise further innovation and efficiency but also pose ethical and privacy concerns. Navigating this landscape requires a continued focus on education and critical engagement with technology, ensuring that progress benefits all members of society equitably.

In conclusion, as the digital revolution unfolds, the Caribbean diaspora stands poised to make significant contributions to the global tapestry of innovation and culture. By leveraging technology, fostering education, and nurturing a spirit of community, the digital age can be a time of unparalleled opportunity and prosperity for the descendants of the Windrush generation and beyond.

Leveraging Technology for Wealth Creation

In an era where the digital landscape dominates, leveraging technology for wealth creation has become an indispensable strategy for not only bridging gaps but also forging new pathways to prosperity. This is especially poignant for the descendants of the Windrush generation, for whom technology offers new platforms to amplify their voices, innovate within their communities, and build economic fortunes that can last for generations.

Understanding the digital revolution's role in wealth creation requires a recognition of its potential to democratize access to opportunities. From e-commerce platforms that empower entrepreneurs to reach global markets to educational resources that make knowledge accessible to all, technology has the power to level the playing field in unprecedented ways.

The rise of fintech, for example, has revolutionized the way individuals and businesses manage their finances, offering tools for budgeting, investing, and transferring money that are more accessible and often less costly than traditional banking services. This innovation holds particular significance for minority communities, where technological solutions can circumvent historical barriers to financial services and literacy.

Social media and digital marketing have also emerged as powerful tools for wealth creation. By harnessing these platforms, businesses owned by the Windrush descendants and others can reach broader audiences without the need for substantial marketing budgets. This democratization of promotional tools allows for a more level competitive field against more established companies.

Moreover, the gig economy, facilitated by technology, has opened up new avenues for earning income. Digital platforms connect freelancers with global opportunities, allowing for flexible and remote work that can be particularly beneficial for those balancing multiple responsibilities or facing employment discrimination in traditional settings.

It's worth noting the educational impact of technology as well. Online courses, webinars, and platforms offer skills training and professional development that are crucial for staying competitive in today's job market. Access to these resources can significantly affect one's ability to create and accumulate wealth.

Despite the optimistic view, it's important to acknowledge the digital divide that can exacerbate existing inequalities. Access to reliable internet and digital literacy remains a challenge for some, highlighting the need for targeted initiatives to ensure that technology serves as a bridge rather than a barrier.

Collaboration between government, private sector, and community organizations can play a pivotal role in addressing these challenges. By investing in digital infrastructure and education, creating policies that support technological innovation, and promoting inclusivity in the tech industry, we can foster an environment where technology truly facilitates wealth creation for all.

Success stories abound, showcasing individuals and businesses that have harnessed technology to not only succeed financially but also contribute to their communities. These stories serve as powerful examples and models for others to follow, offering insights and inspiration for how to effectively leverage technology for wealth creation.

As we look to the future, the potential for technological innovation to continue driving wealth creation is boundless. Emerging technologies like blockchain, artificial intelligence, and the Internet of Things hold promise for creating new industries, transforming existing ones, and providing even more opportunities for economic empowerment.

The journey of the Windrush generation and their descendants is one marked by resilience, innovation, and a relentless pursuit of prosperity and fulfillment. In embracing technology and its potential for wealth creation, this community can continue to break barriers and build legacies that will inspire future generations.

Ultimately, leveraging technology for wealth creation is more than just about economic gain; it's about empowering individuals and communities to realize their full potential. It's about creating a more equitable and prosperous future for all, where the digital landscape serves as fertile ground for innovation, opportunity, and lasting change.

In conclusion, the synergy between technology and wealth creation offers a powerful tool for bridging gaps and forging new paths to prosperity. As we continue to navigate the complexities of the digital age, it's vital to approach technology not just as a means to an end but as an integral part of our collective journey towards economic empowerment and generational wealth. The legacy of the Windrush generation provides a foundation of resilience and innovation on which to build, reminding us of the endless possibilities that await when we leverage technology with purpose and vision.

Chapter 8:
Education and Empowerment:
Keys to Generational Wealth

In the previous chapters, the narrative traced the nuances of resilience, innovation, and the indomitable entrepreneurial spirit of the Windrush generation. As we transition into the realm of education and empowerment, it's vital to recognize these as pivotal instruments in cementing a legacy of generational wealth. The Windrush saga underscores education not merely as a formal learning process but an empowering tool that bridges generations, cultures, and economies. It's the bedrock on which dreams are built and aspirations are realized. Through myriad success stories, this chapter delves into how education, in its various forms, has enabled individuals and communities to transcend socio-economic barriers, fostering environments where creativity thrives and potential is limitless.

Empowerment, on the other hand, is portrayed as the catalyst that propels individuals to leverage their gained knowledge, igniting a cycle of prosperity that cascades through generations. It's an affirmation that beyond the confines of classrooms and textbooks lies the real essence of education –

the awakening of minds, the instilling of hope, and the nurturing of an unyielding belief in one's capabilities. Celebrating this transformative power, the chapter embarks on a journey through the heartwarming tales of those who've wielded education and empowerment as their weapons to carve paths of success, laying the groundwork for a future where generational wealth is not just a possibility but a concrete reality for the descendants of the Windrush voyagers.

The Importance of Education

Education stands as a cornerstone in the edifice of generational wealth, serving not just as a pathway to economic prosperity but as a vital tool for empowerment and social elevation. Throughout history, education has been a transformative force, shaping societies, influencing cultures, and altering the course of individual lives. For the descendants of the Windrush generation, the pursuit of education has been both a mission and a testament to resilience in the face of systemic obstacles.

The narrative of education within the context of generational wealth is not one of mere academic achievement. It is, at its core, a story of liberation and empowerment. Education equips individuals with the knowledge and skills necessary to navigate the complexities of the modern world, fostering innovative thinking and enabling informed decision-making. It enlightens minds, enriches spirits, and emboldens the pursuit of dreams, transforming potential into reality.

In the aftermath of the Windrush arrival, the significance of education became increasingly apparent. It was regarded as the key that could unlock doors previously closed by economic disparity and racial discrimination. The pioneering individuals of this generation recognized that education had the power to dismantle barriers, challenge status quos, and lay the groundwork for a future characterized by prosperity and equality.

However, the journey toward educational attainment was fraught with challenges. The Windrush descendants encountered a British educational system that was often unprepared and sometimes unwilling to meet their needs. Amidst these trials, the community's resolve only strengthened, galvanized by a collective understanding of education's transformative power.

Innovative and community-driven educational strategies emerged as a response. Supplementary schools were established, offering tailored support and fostering a sense of identity and belonging among Caribbean students. These grassroots movements were instrumental in cultivating a generation that would go on to make significant contributions across various sectors.

The ripple effects of these efforts are evident today. Success stories abound, featuring individuals from the Windrush lineage who have excelled in fields as diverse as medicine, law, academia, and the arts. These success stories underscore the premise that education is not merely a personal achievement but a communal asset, a legacy passed from one generation to the next.

The importance of education cannot be overstated when discussing strategies for building generational wealth. It is a critical asset that appreciates over time, immune to the volatility that characterizes financial markets. Its value transcends monetary worth, encompassing social capital, cultural preservation, and the perpetuation of values that champion equity and justice.

Indeed, education acts as a leveller, offering individuals from all backgrounds the opportunity to aspire to and achieve greatness. It has the unique capability to bridge the gap between potential and opportunity, serving as a catalyst for social mobility and economic advancement.

In the context of the Windrush narrative, education represents a powerful act of defiance—an assertion of dignity, rights, and aspirations. It is a declaration that despite systemic challenges, the pursuit of knowledge and the quest for a better life are endeavors worth undertaking.

Empowerment through education extends beyond the individual. It has a multiplier effect, benefiting families, communities, and society at large. Educated individuals are better equipped to contribute to the social, economic, and political fabric of their communities, driving positive change and fostering an environment where future generations can thrive.

As we reflect on the enduring legacy of the Windrush generation, it becomes clear that education is not just a key to unlocking personal potential; it is a foundational pillar supporting the edifice of generational wealth. It is an investment in the future, a means of ensuring that the sacrifices of past generations bear fruit in the lives of those yet to come.

The story of education and empowerment within the Windrush narrative is one of triumph over adversity, a testament to the power of persistence, community, and foresight. It serves as a beacon of hope and a guide for future generations, illuminating the path toward prosperity, fulfillment, and an enduring legacy of wealth well beyond the financial.

In closing, the centrality of education in the quest for generational wealth cannot be overstated. It is a critical tool for empowerment, a means of dismantling systemic barriers, and a vehicle for societal transformation. As we look to the future, let us carry forward the legacy of the Windrush generation, championing education not only as a fundamental human right but as a pivotal force in the creation of a just, equitable, and prosperous society.

In the grand narrative of human progression, education emerges not just as a chapter but as the very thread weaving through the tapestry of history, binding generations together in a shared quest for enlightenment, empowerment, and enduring prosperity. The importance of education, therefore, transcends the immediate—it is the bedrock upon which the dreams of tomorrow are built.

Success Stories and Inspirational Models The journey of the Windrush generation, and indeed their descendants, encapsulates a profound narrative of resilience, innovation, and unwavering pursuit of success against the backdrop of systemic challenges. Within the realm of education and empowerment, several luminous examples emerge, serving not only as beacons of hope but also as concrete proof of the transformative power of education in crafting legacies of generational wealth.

Their stories begin with the foundational belief that education serves as the cornerstone for personal and collective advancement. Among these narratives, the story of Sir Geoff Palmer stands tall. Knighted for his contributions to science, human rights, and charity, Palmer's journey from arriving in the UK as part of the Windrush generation to becoming a leading figure in grain science underscores the pivotal role of education in surmounting socio-economic barriers.

In a similar vein, the achievements of Baroness Floella Benjamin highlight how education, coupled with an ironclad resolve, can propel one from the humble beginnings of a Windrush descendant to influential positions in British society and beyond. Her advocacy for children's rights and education has left indelible marks on policy and practice, showcasing the potential of informed passion to enact transformative change.

Moreover, the path of Professor Dame Elizabeth Anionwu, a pioneering nurse, and educator, reveals the power of education to break the chains of racial and socio-economic limitations. Rising through the ranks from a humble background, her contributions to nursing, particularly in the field of sickle cell disease, spotlight the capacity of educational attainment to spearhead groundbreaking advancements in healthcare.

The educational pursuits of the Windrush generation and their descendants have not only opened doors to personal and professional growth but have also contributed significantly to the social and economic fabric of Britain. As educators, scientists, politicians, and more, their legacies underscore the transformative power of education as a tool for societal advancement and personal fulfillment.

In the context of building generational wealth, these success stories emphasize the importance of investing in one's intellectual and personal growth. They reaffirm that education is not merely a path to economic prosperity but is fundamentally a means of empowerment that enables individuals to navigate, influence, and contribute to the world around them more effectively.

It's imperative to acknowledge that these achievements do not stand in isolation. Behind each success story is a tale of perseverance, resilience, and the strategic use of resources, often in the face of daunting adversity. In this way, the Windrush generation has laid down a roadmap for future generations, illustrating that success is not merely defined by one's starting point but by their vision, determination, and the relentless pursuit of excellence.

Their stories also serve as a clarion call for the significance of mentorship and community support in facilitating educational and professional achievements. The inspirational models of the Windrush generation highlight the impactful role of collective effort in elevating individual success to generational legacies.

In conclusion, the education and empowerment of the Windrush generation and their descendants provide a compelling narrative of triumph over adversity. As current and future generations look to these inspirational models, the lesson is clear: education is an invaluable asset in the journey towards generational wealth, one that requires dedication, resilience, and the unwavering belief in the power of self-advancement.

The legacy of the Windrush generation, therefore, transcends the socio-economic contributions to Britain. It embodies the indomitable spirit of hope, the unwavering pursuit of excellence, and the transformative power of education. As we honor their contributions, we also embrace their legacy as a roadmap for future generations, lighting the way toward prosperity, fulfillment, and lasting impact on society.

Chapter 9:
The Windrush Effect on Modern Diversity Policies

The Windrush generation's arrival on British shores was not merely a footnote in history but a pivotal chapter that reshaped the nation's approach to diversity and inclusion. In the aftermath of their settlement, Britain's socio-political landscapes underwent transformative changes, steering the course towards more inclusive, representative, and equitable systems. The Windrush legacy, deeply imbued with resilience and a quest for justice, became instrumental in the enactment of groundbreaking legislative reforms. These policies not only sought to correct past injustices but also paved the way for a more vibrant, diverse society where cultures intertwine and enrich one another. The evolution of diversity policies, influenced significantly by the Windrush generation's advocacy and its undeniable contribution to the British tapestry, underscores a vital lesson: embracing diversity is not merely an ethical imperative but a cornerstone of societal prosperity and innovation. As we chart the course for future generations, the Windrush spirit continues to inspire policies that foster inclusion, celebrate cultural heritage, and propel communities towards achieving generational wealth and well-being. This chapter, therefore, delves into the profound legacy of the Windrush generation, examining its enduring impact on modern diversity policies and how it has sculpted a more inclusive Britain. Through their journey, we glean insights into the resilience necessary to overcome adversity and the pivotal role of diverse communities in enriching and advancing societies.

Influence on British Socio-Political Landscapes

The upheaval and aftermath of World War II set the stage for monumental changes within the British socio-political frameworks, particularly in the realms of diversity, inclusion, and immigration policies. At the heart of this transformation was the Windrush generation, whose arrival planted the seeds of multicultural Britain we recognize today. This section delves into the profound impact of the Windrush saga on the socio-political landscapes of Britain, shedding light on the journey from mere legislative alterations to the cultivation of an inclusive societal ethos.

In the immediate post-war years, Britain faced a dire need for labor to rebuild a nation ravaged by conflict. The invitation extended to the countries of the British Empire was more than a call for help; it was a beckon for change. As the Windrush generation arrived, their presence gradually challenged and reshaped British perceptions on race, community, and national identity.

Legislatively, the presence of the Windrush settlers spurred the British government into action. The British Nationality Act 1948, which laid the groundwork for Commonwealth citizens to settle in Britain, was the initial step towards acknowledging the shifting demographics. However, the journey towards genuine inclusivity and equality was fraught with resistance and backlash.

Racial tensions flared, notably during the Notting Hill riots of 1958, highlighting the societal challenges faced by the Caribbean community. These episodes revealed the deep-seated prejudices and the need for a comprehensive approach to race relations in Britain. It underscored the urgency for legislation that not only protected the rights of minority groups but also actively promoted racial harmony.

The subsequent decades saw a series of legislative acts aimed at reducing discrimination and fostering a more inclusive society. The Race Relations Act of 1965 marked a pioneering move towards outlawing racial discrimination in public places, a testament to the growing recognition of the need for statutory protections for Britain's diverse population.

Education and public discourse evolved alongside these legislative changes. Schools began to adapt, slowly incorporating lessons that reflected the rich tapestry of the nation's cultural diversity. Media representation followed, albeit at a slower pace, as stories and images of the Caribbean and other minority communities began to thread into the broader narrative of British identity.

In the realm of politics, the Windrush generation and their descendants carved out significant roles. By the late 20th and early 21st centuries, political representation had begun to reflect the multicultural nature of the British populace more accurately. This was not merely a matter of numbers but a profound shift in the political discourse towards inclusivity and understanding.

The influence of the Windrush generation extends beyond the corridors of power and the pages of legislation. It permeates the very essence of British social fabric, encouraging a celebration of diversity that has become quintessentially British. Events like the Notting Hill Carnival have transcended their origins to become symbols of unity and cultural synthesis.

Furthermore, the Windrush scandal of recent years serves as a sobering reminder of the ongoing challenges faced by minority communities in Britain. The fight for justice and recognition for the Windrush generation renewed awareness and commitment to safeguarding the rights of all citizens, particularly those who have been instrumental in shaping modern Britain.

This journey from legislation to inclusion underscores the dynamic nature of socio-political landscapes in Britain, influenced markedly by the Windrush generation. It highlights a progression from tolerance to celebration, from recognition to empowerment. The legislative milestones, while critical, are merely part of a broader narrative of social evolution and communal harmony.

In grappling with its colonial past and the legacies of empire, Britain has found in the Windrush generation a source of renewal and redefinition. The society that has emerged is one that strives to be more equitable, more reflective of its diverse constituents, and more cognizant of its historical complexities.

The Windrush generation's impact on British socio-political landscapes offers a tapestry of lessons in resilience, community, and transformation. It is a testament to the enduring power of migration to reshape societies in profound and lasting ways.

As Britain continues to navigate its future, the influence of the Windrush generation remains a beacon. It serves as a reminder of the complexities of identity, the challenges of integration, and the boundless potential of diversity as a source of societal strength and cohesion.

In conclusion, the journey of the Windrush generation and their indelible mark on the British socio-political landscapes is a narrative of hope, struggle, and triumph. It is a reflection of the broader human experience, emphasizing the importance of inclusion, understanding, and mutual respect. As we look forward, let the legacy of the Windrush generation inspire us to build a society that truly reflects the richness of its diverse voices, cultivating a future where prosperity and fulfillment are accessible to all.

From Legislation to Inclusion As we traverse through the annals of history, the journey from mere legislation to genuine inclusion emerges as a formidable challenge that societies worldwide have endeavored to overcome. The saga of the Windrush generation is emblematic of this quest, showcasing an evolution that, while fraught with adversity, paved the way for a brighter future. The concept of inclusion extends beyond the enfranchisement rendered by laws; it is the fabric of a community that welcomes diversity and harnesses it for mutual prosperity.

The legislative aftermath of the Windrush arrival initiated a slow but significant transformation in the British societal landscape. Initially, laws were enacted to manage migration, often with the underlying intention of restriction. However, as the narratives of the Windrush settlers interwove with the British identity, legislation began to evolve, reflecting a gradual shift towards recognizing the value of multicultural integration.

This transformation was neither swift nor straightforward. Each legislative milestone encountered resistance, both at the institutional level and within the general populace. Yet, it was the indomitable spirit of the Windrush generation that served as a catalyst for change. They demonstrated not only their indispensability to the British economy but also enriched the cultural tapestry of the nation with their vibrant traditions and resilience.

The turning point came with the Race Relations Acts, a series of legislations spanning from the 1960s to the 1970s, designed to tackle racial discrimination. Although not perfect, these laws marked a significant departure from exclusionary practices, laying the legal foundation for inclusion. Yet, it was clear that laws alone could not dismantle entrenched social prejudices or bridge the chasm between legislation and genuine societal acceptance.

The journey towards inclusion required more than legal reforms; it demanded a transformation in societal attitudes. The Windrush generation and their descendants played a pivotal role in this process, leveraging their cultural heritage to foster a deeper understanding and appreciation amongst the broader British public.

Education emerged as a powerful tool in this endeavor, not only in the formal sense but also through the informal education that comes from community interaction, cultural exchange, and shared experiences. Through these interactions, barriers began to erode, and the seeds of inclusion were sown.

Economic contributions were equally significant in altering perceptions. As members of the Windrush generation established businesses, they underscored their role as key contributors to the British economy. These entrepreneurial ventures did more than provide livelihoods; they served as bridges between diverse communities, enabling a more profound social integration.

Artistic expressions, particularly music and literature, offered another avenue through which the Windrush settlers and their descendants shaped British culture. The calypso rhythms and reggae beats, once foreign, became synonymous with the British music scene, epitomizing the fusion of cultures that lay at the heart of the inclusion journey.

Despite these strides towards inclusion, challenges persist. Discrimination and social inequalities remain obstacles that the Windrush descendants continue to navigate. The inclusion journey is ongoing, marked by victories and setbacks alike, reminding us that the path to a truly inclusive society is a marathon, not a sprint.

Yet, hope endures, fueled by the relentless pursuit of equality and the enduring legacy of the Windrush generation. Their story epitomizes the strength found in diversity and the potential for unity in the face of adversity. It serves as a beacon of hope for subsequent generations, emphasizing that inclusion is not just a distant ideal but a tangible goal within reach.

The narrative of the Windrush generation thus transcends the boundaries of history; it is a living testament to the power of resilience, the importance of community, and the unyielding belief in the promise of inclusion. Their journey from legislative recognition to genuine societal acceptance illustrates a fundamental truth: inclusion enriches not only the lives of those embraced but the fabric of society as a whole.

As we look to the future, the lessons gleaned from this saga of inclusion will undoubtedly shape the strategies to combat discrimination and foster a truly inclusive society. It is a journey that requires collective effort, unwavering commitment, and an understanding that our differences, when united, form our greatest strength.

In the final analysis, the transition from legislation to inclusion underscores a poignant narrative of human endurance and the unrelenting pursuit of a society where everyone, irrespective of their background, is valued and included. The Windrush generation laid the groundwork for this vision, challenging us to continue their legacy of resilience and hope. It is a call to action for future generations, urging them to weave the principles of diversity, equity, and inclusion into the very fabric of their lives and communities.

In embracing this challenge, we honor the Windrush legacy and contribute to creating a world that celebrates diversity as a source of strength and inclusion as the cornerstone of prosperity. It is a journey worth undertaking, promising a future where the wealth of experiences and perspectives unite to forge a society that is truly inclusive. For in the heart of inclusion lies the essence of humanity: the recognition that within each of us is the potential to contribute to, and indeed enrich, the tapestry of our collective existence.

Chapter 10:
Preserving Culture and
Tradition Amidst Innovation

In the dynamic interplay of progress and preservation, the Windrush generation stands as a testament to the resilience of cultural heritage against the tides of innovation. This chapter delves into the intricate balance between embracing modern advancements and safeguarding the rich tapestry of traditions that define a community's identity. It's a landscape where community organizations become the custodians of heritage, meticulously weaving the threads of the past with the aspirations of the future. Through festivals, oral histories, and diasporic networks, these groups ensure that the essence of Caribbean culture not only survives but flourishes, amidst a world that's constantly evolving. Such efforts highlight a profound truth: that in the heart of innovation lies the potential to enhance, rather than eclipse, the cultural legacy that forms the backbone of a community's wealth. Celebrating heritage while looking forward renders a dazzling spectrum of possibilities, where the wisdom of yore and the innovations of tomorrow exist in harmony. This chapter aims to inspire by showcasing how the preservation of culture and tradition amidst the whirlwind of innovation is not just possible but vital. It serves as a beacon, guiding future generations on a journey where prosperity encompasses both the wealth of the pocket and the richness of the soul.

The Role of Community Organizations

As we delve into the profound significance of community organizations in preserving culture and tradition amidst innovation, it becomes evident that these entities serve as the backbone of cultural transmission. In every culture, certain institutions play a pivotal role in the preservation of heritage, and for the Windrush generation and their descendants, community organizations have been indispensable in this endeavor. These organizations provide a space where culture is not only preserved but also celebrated and evolved in alignment with contemporary realities.

At the heart of these organizations lies the principle of unity. Community organizations act as a gathering place for people with shared experiences, histories, and aspirations. They offer a sanctuary where traditions are taught, practiced, and passed down through generations. Such entities become crucial at a time when mainstream narratives often overlook or misinterpret the nuances of specific cultural heritages. Through events, workshops, and educational programs, community organizations ensure that culture is a living, breathing concept that connects individuals with their ancestors' wisdom while navigating the challenges of the modern world.

Moreover, amidst the rapid pace of innovation, community organizations provide the necessary balance between embracing technological advancements and maintaining cultural authenticity. They demonstrate that innovation is not a departure from tradition but rather a tool through which tradition can be reinterpreted and reinvigorated. By integrating new technologies with traditional practices, these organizations make culture accessible and relevant to younger generations, ensuring its survival and continued relevance.

In this age of globalization, community organizations also play a critical role in creating a sense of belonging among diaspora communities. As people migrate and establish themselves in new lands, the risk of cultural dilution becomes a pressing concern. Community organizations stand in the gap, offering a bridge back to one's roots while also providing a platform for cultural exchange and mutual understanding among diverse populations. This unique position enables them to foster a global appreciation of Windrush culture and traditions, promoting a world that values diversity and inclusivity.

Additionally, the mentorship and support networks found within these community organizations are invaluable. They serve not only as custodians of tradition but also as beacons of support, guiding individuals as they navigate the complexities of identity in a multicultural context. Within their walls, young and old alike find guidance, encouragement, and inspiration, drawing strength from their shared heritage to pursue success in various spheres of life.

Community organizations also embody resilience and resistance. Through their existence and activities, they contest narratives of marginalization and demonstrate the vibrancy, complexity, and dynamism of their cultures. Celebrations, festivals, and other cultural events become acts of defiance against cultural erasure, making visible the contributions and significance of their community in the broader social tapestry.

Furthermore, these organizations are pivotal in promoting intergenerational dialogue. They create spaces where elders and youth can engage in meaningful conversations, sharing stories, skills, and knowledge. This exchange is crucial for the preservation of intangible cultural heritage, such as oral histories, music, dance, and linguistic nuances, which are often not captured in books or artifacts but are alive within the people.

In the sphere of economic development, community organizations encourage entrepreneurship and economic empowerment within their communities. By supporting culturally relevant businesses, they not only foster economic prosperity but also ensure that the marketplace reflects the diversity of the community's cultural landscape. This economic dimension adds a tangible value to cultural preservation, demonstrating that culture and tradition can coexist and even thrive alongside innovation.

Education plays a central role in the efforts of community organizations to preserve culture and tradition. Through tailored educational initiatives, children and adults alike are immersed in the richness of their cultural heritage. Language classes, history lessons, and cultural competency workshops become tools through which individuals can deeply understand and appreciate their identity and heritage.

These organizations often collaborate with local and national governments, advocating for policies and initiatives that support cultural preservation and recognition. Through advocacy, they ensure that the voices of their communities are heard, influencing policy decisions that affect their cultural rights and heritage.

Environmental sustainability is another lens through which community organizations approach cultural preservation. Recognizing the deep connections between culture, tradition, and the natural world, these organizations often lead efforts in ecological conservation. By promoting sustainable practices rooted in traditional knowledge, they highlight the relevance of cultural wisdom in addressing contemporary environmental challenges.

The role of community organizations in preserving culture and tradition amidst innovation is multifaceted and profound. They act as custodians of culture, educators, advocates, and bridge builders. By weaving together the threads of tradition and innovation, they ensure that culture remains a vibrant and dynamic force that enriches the lives of individuals and communities alike.

In conclusion, the significance of community organizations cannot be overstated. They are crucial in ensuring that as we embrace the future, we do not lose sight of our past. They remind us that in our rapidly changing world, our cultures and traditions are not relics of a bygone era but are, in fact, essential components of our collective identity and prosperity. Through their efforts, the legacy of the Windrush generation and the richness of their heritage will continue to inspire and guide future generations.

As we move forward, let us support and champion the work of these community organizations. Through collective action, advocacy, and support, we can ensure that our cultural heritage continues to flourish, providing a foundation of strength, unity, and resilience for generations to come. The journey of preserving culture and tradition amidst innovation is not easy, but it is undoubtedly noble and vital for the enrichment of the human spirit and the tapestry of global culture.

Celebrating Heritage while Looking Forward As we delve into the substantive depths of the Windrush generation's influence, we encounter an enduring thread of resilience, hope, and the audacious spirit of innovation. This chapter is a testament to the indomitable will of those who, despite facing adversity, remained anchored in their heritage while simultaneously charting a course for the future. The essence of this narrative is not merely to acknowledge the past but to illuminate the paths these pioneers have laid for succeeding generations.

The narrative of the Windrush generation is a striking illustration of how adversity can foster a breeding ground for innovation and creativity. These individuals, who had voyaged across the ocean, brought with them not just the tangible aspects of their culture but also an intangible legacy of resilience, determination, and the ability to adapt and innovate in the face of adversity. This chapter explores various dimensions of how the Windrush generation preserved their heritage while contributing significantly to the cultural and economic landscape of their new homeland.

The celebration of heritage by the Windrush generation involved more than the mere preservation of cultural traditions. It represented a dynamic interplay between retaining a sense of identity and engaging with, contributing to, and indeed transforming, the cultural and social fabric of Britain. Through their culinary traditions, music, literature, and religious practices, they not only maintained their Caribbean identity but also introduced Britons to a vibrantly diverse culture.

Music, in particular, played a pivotal role in this cultural exchange. Calypso and later reggae served as powerful mediums of expression for the Windrush generation, narrating stories of their experiences, struggles, and hopes. These musical genres transcended entertainment, becoming symbols of resistance and instruments of cultural integration. Through music, the Windrush pioneers communicated their narrative, shared their heritage, and fostered a greater understanding among diverse communities.

Another significant contribution of the Windrush generation to their adopted homeland was in the realm of entrepreneurship. Faced with systemic barriers in employment, many within the community turned to create their businesses, thereby carving out spaces of economic independence and innovation. From culinary ventures that introduced Caribbean flavors to the British palate to the establishment of community centers that served as hubs for cultural preservation and social support, these entrepreneurial efforts were instrumental in both sustaining the community and enriching the broader society.

Furthermore, the realm of literature and the arts saw influential contributions from the Windrush generation, with writers and artists drawing upon their experiences and heritage to produce works that challenged prevailing narratives and offered new perspectives. Through their artistic expressions, they fostered dialogue, increased visibility for marginalized voices, and contributed to the rich tapestry of British culture.

The importance of education cannot be understated in the pursuit of preserving culture while pursuing prosperity. Members of the Windrush generation placed a high value on education, both as a means of personal advancement and as a way to contribute to and engage with their community and broader society. This emphasis on education has been passed down through generations, serving as a cornerstone for building generational wealth and fostering a culture of innovation and entrepreneurial spirit.

As we look to the future, it's imperative to recognize the significance of technology as a tool for both preserving heritage and fostering innovation. The digital age offers unprecedented opportunities for the Caribbean diaspora to connect, share their stories, and engage in entrepreneurial ventures that can reach a global audience. Leveraging technology, future generations have the potential to further bridge the gap between celebrating heritage and achieving economic prosperity.

The Windrush legacy, while deeply rooted in the past, offers a shining beacon for the future. It exemplifies the power of resilience, the importance of community, and the transformative potential of embracing one's heritage while innovating for the future. This chapter serves as a reminder that the journey embarked upon by the Windrush generation is far from complete; it continues in the lives of those who follow, imbued with the spirit of innovation and the richness of their heritage.

Community organizations have played and continue to play, a crucial role in preserving the cultural heritage of the Windrush generation while fostering innovation and economic growth. These entities not only serve as custodians of traditions and history but also as catalysts for community development and empowerment. They exemplify the collective effort required to sustain cultural identity while embracing the opportunities presented by a changing world.

In celebrating the heritage of the Windrush generation while looking forward, it's essential to recognize the intertwined nature of cultural preservation and economic advancement. The legacy of the Windrush generation teaches us that prosperity is not merely about economic success but also about the richness of one's cultural identity and the strength of community ties. It challenges us to envision a future where embracing our heritage is seen as a foundation for innovation and growth.

The resilience and creativity of the Windrush generation have left an indelible mark on society, challenging us to consider how we can honor their legacy in our own lives. By nurturing the values of community, innovation, and resilience, we can strive to build a future that reflects the best of our diverse heritage while forging paths toward prosperity and fulfillment.

As we reflect on the journey of the Windrush generation and their contribution to our shared history, we are reminded of the power of hope and the enduring strength of the human spirit. Their story is a testament to the fact that, even in the face of formidable obstacles, it is possible to celebrate one's heritage while making significant strides forward.

The narrative of the Windrush generation is not just a chapter in history; it is a continuous source of inspiration and a roadmap for future generations. It encourages us to embrace our heritage with pride, to face challenges with courage, and to innovate with the conviction that our contributions can indeed shape a brighter future.

Ultimately, "Celebrating Heritage while Looking Forward" encapsulates a vital message for all of us, irrespective of our background or origin. It highlights the importance of recognizing and honoring our cultural heritage as a source of strength, inspiration, and innovation. As we take up the mantle from the Windrush generation, let us commit to fostering a legacy that blends the richness of our past with the boundless possibilities of our future, paving the way for prosperity and fulfillment for generations to come.

Chapter 11:
The Road Ahead: Lessons
for Future Generations

As we stand at the precipice of the future, gazing out over the vast expanse of possibilities, the lessons of the Windrush generation serve as both a compass and a beacon, guiding us towards a future ripe with potential for prosperity and fulfillment. The resilience, innovation, and determination demonstrated by this remarkable group of individuals have laid a solid foundation upon which future generations can build. We have learned that the journey towards generational wealth is not merely about the accumulation of financial assets, but rather it's about cultivating a legacy of wisdom, courage, and perseverance. It's about embracing our cultural heritage while innovating for the future. As we move forward, let us remember the importance of education as a powerful tool for empowerment, the value of creativity in overcoming adversity, and the significance of community in sustaining our achievements. The road ahead is filled with opportunities for those who dare to dream and have the courage to act. Let us proceed with the understanding that our actions today will shape the legacy we leave for the generations that follow, inspiring them to reach new heights and continue the cycle of wealth and well-being that was so bravely forged by the Windrush generation.

Embracing the Legacy

In traversing the annals of history, one can't help but marvel at the resilience of the Windrush generation, whose narrative of hope, excitement, and, ultimately, triumph has left an indelible mark on the tapestry of modern society. The legacy of this formidable generation is not merely a tale of past endeavors but a guiding light, illuminating the path for future generations. As we delve into the essence of embracing this legacy, it becomes evident that the lessons imprinted by the Windrush generation are far-reaching, touching the realms of prosperity, innovation, and cultural preservation.

The Windrush voyage—a journey emblematic of the pursuit for a better life—encapsulates the essence of determination and courage. The decision to leave familiar shores for the unknown was not taken lightly; it was a testament to the unyielding spirit of those eager to contribute to a society recovering from the ravages of war. Their arrival heralded a new chapter, not just for the immigrants themselves but for the very fabric of British society, which would be forever altered.

Beyond the shores of Britain, the West Indian contribution transcended economic reconstruction; it sowed the seeds for a cultural renaissance that would challenge the monolithic narrative of British identity. The integration of West Indian culture—its music, culinary delights, and literature—served to enrich the cultural landscape, fostering an environment of diversity and innovation.

The concept of generational wealth, though often associated with financial assets, takes on a broader significance in the context of the Windrush legacy. It encompasses the wealth of knowledge, cultural heritage, and the spirit of resilience passed down through the generations. This multifaceted inheritance underscores the importance of preserving history while forging ahead with innovation.

Indeed, the spirit of innovation was markedly evident among the Windrush generation. Facing the dual challenges of racial discrimination and economic marginalization, they carved out spaces for themselves, transforming survival strategies into prosperous ventures. Their innovative approaches to building a life in a new land highlight the capacity for creativity amidst adversity.

The essence of creativity, particularly in the realm of art and culture, became a medium through which the Windrush generation articulated their narrative, shaping the multicultural tapestry of Britain. From the vibrant rhythms of calypso music to the poignant narratives told through literature and art, they asserted their identity and contribution to society.

Entrepreneurship and economic innovation were also hallmarks of this generation's legacy. Despite encountering significant barriers, West Indian businesses flourished, contributing to the economic vibrancy of their communities and beyond. Their entrepreneurial spirit serves as an inspiring model for future generations.

The advent of the digital era ushered in new opportunities for bridging gaps and fostering innovation. The legacy of the Windrush generation, with its emphasis on adaptability and resilience, provides invaluable lessons in leveraging technology for wealth creation, cultural preservation, and community building.

Education emerged as a cornerstone of generational wealth, a means through which future generations could attain empowerment and prosperity. The stories of individuals who, against all odds, pursued higher education and succeeded, serve as powerful testaments to the transformative power of knowledge and perseverance.

The impact of the Windrush generation on modern diversity policies cannot be overstated. Their presence and the subsequent socio-cultural integration played a pivotal role in shaping inclusive legislation and policies, laying the groundwork for a more diverse and equitable society.

In the endeavor to preserve culture and tradition amidst the waves of innovation, community organizations have played a crucial role. These entities, embodying the communal spirit of the Windrush generation, stand as beacons of heritage, ensuring that the rich tapestry of West Indian culture continues to flourish.

The path laid down by the Windrush generation is one marked by resilience, innovation, and a profound sense of community. As we look to the future, it is incumbent upon us to embrace this legacy, drawing upon its lessons to navigate the complexities of modern society. The journey ahead, though fraught with challenges, offers endless possibilities for growth, fulfillment, and the continued enrichment of our diverse cultural landscape.

The roadmap for prosperity and fulfillment, as illuminated by the Windrush legacy, hinges on the principles of innovation, education, and the preservation of cultural heritage. It invites each of us to reflect on our own contributions to the fabric of society, encouraging a collective effort toward the betterment of humanity.

In embracing the Windrush legacy, we not only honor the contributions of past generations but also lay the foundation for a future rich in diversity, innovation, and unity. The lessons they have bequeathed us serve as a clarion call to forge ahead with purpose, resilience, and an unwavering belief in the power of community.

As we stand on the shoulders of giants, the road ahead beckons, filled with the promise of a future crafted by the hands of those who dare to dream, innovate, and persevere. The Windrush legacy, with its rich tapestry of experiences and lessons, serves as our guiding star, lighting the way forward for generations to come.

Innovation as a Tool for Prosperity As we embark on the penultimate narrative of this compelling saga, our focus shifts to innovation, a catalyst for prosperity throughout the chapters of history and within the lives of the Windrush generation. Innovation, in its essence, is the alchemy that transforms challenges into opportunities, enabling individuals and communities to pave pathways to prosperity.

Within this parlous journey, the Windrush generation showcased an unparalleled ability to adapt and innovate, reflecting an indomitable spirit of resilience. The profound lesson at the heart of their experience is that innovation isn't merely a tool for economic gain; it's a mechanism for social and communal transformation. This critical insight serves as a beacon of hope, illuminating the potential for future generations to carve out their destinies through ingenuity and creativity.

Facing the harsh winds of adversity, the Windrush settlers ventured into uncharted territories, pioneering in realms previously unimagined. Their initial struggle was a testament to the power of innovation as a means of survival. Yet, what began as a necessity soon evolved into a strategic approach towards achieving prosperity. It is this evolutionary journey from survival to prosperity that underscores the transformative power of innovative thinking.

In the realms of entrepreneurship, many from the Windrush generation broke new ground, establishing businesses that not only catered to the niche needs of their communities but also appealed to broader markets. These enterprises ranged from culinary ventures that introduced Caribbean flavors to the British palate, to music studios that became the birthplaces of genre-blending sounds. Each endeavor symbolized an act of innovation, turning cultural heritage into economic assets.

The resilience and ingenuity displayed by these pioneers underscore the critical role of creativity in overcoming adversity. This creativity wasn't confined to the sphere of business alone but extended to the arts, where the Windrush generation left an indelible mark. The calypso music of the Caribbean, with its compelling narratives and rhythms, found a new home in Britain, becoming a powerful medium for cultural expression and solidarity.

Innovation within this context was a communal endeavor, with knowledge, skills, and resources often shared within the diaspora network. This culture of communal innovation exemplified the collective effort in building bridges to prosperity, highlighting the significance of unity and collaboration in achieving shared goals.

Moreover, the legacy of the Windrush generation encompasses a profound understanding of the role of education in unlocking the doors to innovation. The empowerment that comes through education enabled many to navigate their way through societal barriers, laying the groundwork for generational wealth built upon knowledge, skills, and innovative thinking.

The digital revolution opened new avenues for the Caribbean diaspora to connect, collaborate, and create. It fostered a global network that transcended geographic limitations, enabling the exchange of ideas and resources at an unprecedented scale. This digital connectivity has been pivotal in leveraging technology for wealth creation, exemplifying innovation's adaptability and its potential to redefine prosperity.

As we delve deeper into the essence of innovation within the Windrush narrative, it's evident that it extends beyond economic measures. Innovation is a reflection of cultural adaptability, a testament to human resilience, and a tribute to the power of imagination. It is through this lens that we perceive innovation as an integral component of the legacy we strive to preserve and propagate.

The journey of the Windrush generation teaches us that innovation isn't simply about inventing new products or services; it's about reimagining the future. It's a clarion call to future generations to harness the power of innovation, to envision and construct a future that pays homage to the past while paving the way for a prosperous tomorrow.

As this chapter concludes, it's imperative to recognize that innovation, as practiced by the Windrush generation, is not merely a historical footnote. It's a guiding principle for all who seek to build a legacy of prosperity. It's a testament to the fact that when confronted with adversity, innovation provides a beacon of hope, a tool for transformation, and a pathway to prosperity.

The narrative of the Windrush generation is replete with instances where innovation transcended economic paradigms, fostering community cohesion, cultural preservation, and societal progress. These endeavors remind us that prosperity, in its truest form, encompasses well-being, fulfillment, and the empowerment of communities.

In embracing their legacy, we are reminded of the profound impact of innovative thinking on human progress. It highlights the importance of viewing challenges as platforms for innovation, encouraging us to approach the future with a mindset that blends creativity with resilience.

The roadmap laid down by the Windrush generation, illuminated by their innovative spirit, inspires us to envision a future rich with possibilities. It beckons us to continue the journey of innovation, using it as a tool not only for achieving prosperity but for forging a legacy that endures for generations to come.

As we approach the closing chapters of this saga, let us carry forward the torch of innovation, inspired by the legacy of those who traversed oceans in search of a brighter tomorrow. Their journey exemplifies the transformative power of innovation, serving as a guiding light for all who aspire to build a future defined by prosperity, resilience, and boundless creativity.

Chapter 12:
Global Impact: The Windrush Legacy Beyond Britain

The indomitable spirit shown by the Windrush generation has resonated far beyond the shores of Britain, embedding itself into the global narrative of migration, determination, and cultural exchange. In this chapter, we delve into how their legacy has transcended national borders, influencing not just the cultural fabric of other nations but also their economies, social policies, and arts. The Windrush saga is a testament to the undeniable strength that lies in diversity and the unforeseen benefits that arise when communities embrace rather than exclude. This diaspora's journey from the Caribbean to Britain and thereafter, to the rest of the world, serves as a powerful model for understanding the contributions migrants make to global society. It challenges us to reconsider notions of nationality and citizenship, urging a reevaluation of what truly constitutes a nation's wealth. The migration patterns triggered by the Windrush generation have paved the way for a remarkable exchange of ideas, traditions, and innovations, significantly enriching various sectors worldwide, from music and cuisine to technology and entrepreneurship. As we continue to navigate the complexities of a rapidly globalizing world, the legacy of the Windrush generation offers guiding principles of resilience, adaptability, and the transformative power of embracing one's heritage while contributing to the common good. This chapter aims to inspire and motivate, reminding us of the profound impact that a group of determined individuals can have on the world stage, forging paths of prosperity and fulfillment for future generations.

Contributions to Global Culture and Economy

The Windrush generation, with their unyielding spirit and determination, has not only shaped the cultural and economic landscape of Britain but has also made indelible marks on the global stage. Their journey, beginning in 1948, was not merely a voyage across the Atlantic; it was the start of a transformation that would ripple through generations and across continents.

In the realm of culture, the influence of the Windrush generation is both profound and far-reaching. They brought with them a rich tapestry of Caribbean culture, infusing the music, food, and literary worlds with vibrant colors, rhythms, and flavors. The global music scene, for example, was forever changed by the introduction of calypso and later reggae, genres that found their roots in the Caribbean but grew in popularity worldwide, thanks to the diaspora.

Moreover, the impact of the Windrush generation extends into the culinary world, where Caribbean cuisine has grown in popularity, transcending geographical and cultural boundaries. Restaurants serving traditional dishes like jerk chicken and roti can now be found in major cities across the world, testimony to the global appetite for the rich flavors of the Caribbean.

On the economic front, members of the Windrush generation have contributed significantly to the economies of their adopted homes and beyond. By taking on jobs in various sectors, from healthcare to transportation, they not only helped rebuild post-war Britain but also laid the groundwork for future generations within the diaspora to excel in entrepreneurial ventures. Their resilience and work ethic have been a driving force behind the establishment and success of numerous West Indian businesses around the globe.

The expression of creativity and innovation among the Windrush generation has been another cornerstone of their legacy. Facing adversity and discrimination, they turned to creativity as a mode of survival, birthing new artistic movements, literary works, and fashion trends that have gained international acclaim over the decades.

Furthermore, the Windrush generation's commitment to education and empowerment has had a lasting impact on global society. Recognizing the value of education as a tool for advancement, many within the community emphasized its importance to their children and communities, leading to a significant number of success stories in academia, business, and professional fields. This emphasis on education has inspired countless individuals around the world to pursue their aspirations despite challenging circumstances.

Their contributions have not been limited to tangible outputs alone. The Windrush generation has played a key role in shaping policies and discussions around diversity, integration, and multiculturalism on an international scale. Through their struggles and successes, they have highlighted the importance of inclusivity and the strength that lies in diversity, influencing policies and practices in numerous countries.

Moreover, the spirit of the Windrush generation has inspired a wave of activism that transcends borders, advocating for the rights and recognition of immigrants around the world. Their legacy serves as a beacon for ongoing struggles for justice and equality, reminding us of the power of resilience and the importance of fighting for a fair and equitable society.

In the realm of sports, the Windrush generation and their descendants have made significant contributions, breaking barriers and setting records in various disciplines. Their achievements have not only brought honor to their communities but have also paved the way for younger athletes of Caribbean descent globally.

Technology and innovation have also felt the impact of the Windrush legacy. From pioneering in digital spaces to leading cutting-edge research, individuals from the Windrush lineage continue to drive progress and innovation, building on the foundation laid by their forebears.

One cannot overlook the role of the Windrush generation in fostering global networks and connections. Through their migration and subsequent activities, they have created a web of relationships that span the globe, facilitating cultural exchange, commerce, and mutual support among diaspora communities.

The influence of the Windrush generation is also evident in the global festival scene, where Caribbean carnivals and other cultural festivities have become highlights in calendars around the world. These events not only celebrate the rich heritage of the Caribbean but also provide an opportunity for diverse communities to come together in unity and festivity.

As mentors and role models, members of the Windrush generation have inspired future generations to dream big and chase their goals relentlessly. Their stories of perseverance and achievement in the face of adversity serve as powerful motivation for young people everywhere, encouraging them to contribute positively to their societies.

Finally, the global impact of the Windrush generation is a testament to the strength and resilience of the human spirit. They have shown that, even in the face of immense challenges, it is possible to create a lasting legacy that enriches not only oneself but also the wider world.

In conclusion, the contributions of the Windrush generation to global culture and economy are vast and deeply ingrained in the fabric of societies around the world. They have paved the way for future generations, setting an example of how determination, hard work, and a commitment to community can overcome challenges and make a lasting difference. As we look forward, their legacy serves as a beacon of hope, inspiring us all to strive for a better, more inclusive world.

A Model for Diaspora Contributions Worldwide
Within the scope of the global diaspora, the concept of

contributing one's skills, resources, and culture back to their homeland or adopted country paints a vivid picture of the boundless potentials unlocked through migration. The diaspora experience, especially that of the Windrush generation, embodies a tremendous value proposition, offering lessons and strategies for diaspora communities worldwide.

The Windrush generation, despite facing insurmountable odds, managed to create a legacy of economic, social, and cultural wealth that continues to inspire. This narrative not only heralds the importance of resilience and innovation but also showcases a model for how diaspora groups can contribute to the socioeconomic fabrics of both their home and host countries. As we delve deeper, the significance of these contributions offers a roadmap for future generations, highlighting the potential to foster prosperity and wider societal benefits through the active engagement of diaspora networks.

Firstly, the economic contributions of the diaspora cannot be overstated. Remittances sent home by diaspora communities assist in alleviating poverty, supporting education, and nurturing small business ventures. The Windrush generation's contribution is a prime example, as it provided much-needed labor for the post-war reconstruction of Britain, significantly aiding economic recovery. This model of contribution demonstrates the dual value diaspora populations can add, boosting the economy of the host country while simultaneously supporting the economic stability of their countries of origin.

Furthermore, the social contributions of the diaspora enrich the cultural tapestry of host countries. Through the diffusion of diverse customs, traditions, and lifestyles, societies become more inclusive, and multicultural understanding deepens. The Caribbean festivals, music, and culinary delights introduced by the Windrush generation have been instrumental in shaping Britain's cultural landscape, underscoring the enriching influence of diaspora contributions.

Educationally, diaspora communities often emphasize the importance of learning and innovation as pathways to success. The Windrush legacy encompasses a strong emphasis on education as a means of empowerment and upward mobility. By investing in education for future generations, diaspora communities lay the groundwork for sustained prosperity, contributing valuable skills and knowledge to their host societies.

Political engagement and activism by diaspora communities have also played a pivotal role in shaping policies and fostering diversity and inclusion in host countries. The Windrush generation's struggles and victories against racial discrimination and inequality have contributed to the evolution of modern diversity policies, illustrating the influential power of diaspora voices in advocating for social justice and change.

Moreover, diaspora communities often lead by example in the realms of entrepreneurship and innovation. Faced with the necessity to adapt to new environments, many from the Windrush generation embarked on entrepreneurial ventures, establishing businesses that filled niche market needs. This entrepreneurial spirit showcases the diaspora's capacity to drive economic innovation, creating jobs and spurring economic growth.

The importance of maintaining cultural heritage while embracing the potential for innovation and adaptation cannot be overlooked. Community organizations play a crucial role in preserving traditions and providing support networks for diaspora communities. The balance of holding onto one's cultural roots while navigating and contributing to a new societal context is pivotal in the success and integration of diaspora populations.

Technology and digital innovation offer new avenues for diaspora contributions. The Windrush generation laid the groundwork, and descendants have the opportunity to leverage technology for even greater impact. By connecting diaspora communities through digital platforms, knowledge transfer, investment, and support mechanisms can be enhanced, further solidifying the economic and social contributions to their respective countries.

It is this multifaceted approach to diaspora contributions, from cultural enrichment and social advocacy to economic investments and educational advancements, that underscores the potential for remarkable impact on global societies. Each contribution, though distinct, reflects a shared ethos of resilience and a commitment to fostering prosperity across generations.

As such, the Windrush example serves as a beacon, illuminating the possibilities that emerge when diaspora communities engage actively with their host and home countries. The lessons gleaned point towards a synergistic relationship between migration and societal advancement, where the contributions of diaspora populations enrich not only their own communities but also the broader global landscape.

To harness the true potential of diaspora contributions, a collaborative approach is essential. Policymakers, community leaders, and individuals must work together to create environments that celebrate diversity, encourage innovation, and facilitate the positive impact of diaspora communities worldwide. Through such collaborative efforts, the legacy of the Windrush generation can be extended, inspiring future generations to contribute to a more prosperous and inclusive world.

In conclusion, the model for diaspora contributions worldwide as exemplified by the Windrush generation is not merely a historical account but a living blueprint for future action. It reminds us of the power of community, the importance of resilience, and the endless opportunities that arise when we embrace the full spectrum of our diverse experiences. By drawing inspiration from the past and applying these lessons to the present, we pave the way for a future where diaspora contributions continue to drive global progress and prosperity.

In the spirit of the Windrush legacy, let us acknowledge the collective strength found within our diverse narratives. May we remain steadfast in our efforts to build bridges of understanding, foster economic empowerment, and promote cultural exchange. It is in this endeavor that we not only honor the contributions of the past but also chart a hopeful course for the vibrant tapestry of humanity that defines our world.

Chapter 13:
The Windrush Legacy -
A Beacon for Tomorrow

As we turn the final pages of this exploration, it becomes evident that the story of the Windrush generation is far more than a historic recounting of a singular voyage. It is a narrative imbued with lessons of courage, innovation, and resilience that continue to resonate through the generations. The Windrush legacy, with its profound implications on wealth, culture, and identity, beckons us to look forward with optimism and a renewed sense of purpose.

The Windrush saga teaches us the integral value of embracing our multifaceted identities and the richness that cultural blending brings to societies. It compels us to acknowledge the indomitable spirit of those who, despite facing insurmountable odds, carved out spaces for themselves and their communities, thereby laying down the foundations for future prosperity. This book has endeavored to map out how these endeavors have not merely contributed to personal gains but have significantly impacted the British economy and its societal fabric.

By delineating the concept of generational wealth within the context of the Windrush experience, we uncover a broader understanding of wealth that transcends monetary assets. It's about fostering an environment where education, empowerment, and equity flourish. It's about creating a legacy of knowledge, values, and opportunities that can be passed down through generations. This nuanced perspective on wealth holds the promise of long-lasting prosperity and fulfillment that is not solely tethered to the accumulation of material wealth.

The spirit of innovation and entrepreneurship demonstrated by the Windrush generation showcases the potent blend of creativity and resilience. Their ability to pivot, adapt, and thrive in unfriendly terrains serves as a powerful blueprint for current and forthcoming generations. In a world that is rapidly evolving, their pioneering approach to challenges and opportunities outlines a path towards achieving sustainable growth and wealth creation.

The elevation of West Indian culture to global stages emphasizes the universal appeal and adaptability of their artistic expressions. It illustrates that in the midst of adversity, creativity burgeons, offering a means of resistance, preservation, and assertion of identity. This cultural legacy, enriched by the Windrush journey, underscores the pivotal role of arts in societal transformation and intercultural dialogue.

The narratives of the entrepreneurs who emerged from this cohort are not just success stories but are testaments to the fact that barriers can be breached. Their tales serve as inspirational beacons that illuminate the pathways of enterprise for others to follow. Understanding their journeys helps underscore the pivotal role of community, innovation, and resilience in the pursuit of economic success and generational wealth.

The digital revolution has opened new vistas for the Caribbean diaspora to connect, collaborate, and contribute to their homeland's development while solidifying their stake in the global marketplace. This convergence of technology and culture is a crucial lever in amplifying the Windrush legacy, ensuring that their contributions continue to resonate and inspire across the globe.

Education remains the cornerstone upon which generational wealth can be built and sustained. By emphasizing the value of learning and empowerment, as demonstrated through the success stories within the Windrush community, we lay bare an essential truth: knowledge and education are indispensable tools in the pursuit of prosperity and well-being.

As we reflect on the modern implications of the Windrush legacy, it becomes clear that their journey has laid a framework for embracing diversity, fostering inclusivity, and advocating for social justice. The strides made in reshaping policies and attitudes towards immigration and multiculturalism owe much to the resilience and activism of the Windrush generation and their descendants.

In conclusion, the Windrush legacy is not relegated to the annals of history but continues to be a vibrant and living testament to human perseverance, innovation, and the quest for justice and equality. It stands as a beacon for tomorrow, guiding us towards a future where wealth is measured not just in financial terms but in the richness of our cultures, the depth of our identities, and the strength of our communities. By embracing the lessons of the past, we can forge a path that honors this legacy and builds a brighter, more inclusive future for all.

Appendix:
Further Reading and Resources

In our journey through the pages of history and the profound legacy of the Windrush generation, we've explored how resilience, innovation, and community can pave the way to generational wealth and societal impact. The narrative doesn't end here, though. There's a wealth of knowledge and inspiration waiting to be discovered by those eager to delve deeper into these topics and continue on their path of learning and growth. Below, you'll find a carefully curated list of books, documentaries, and online resources that expand on the themes explored in this book and offer further fuel for your journey.

Books

"Windrush: The Irresistible Rise of Multi-Racial Britain" by Trevor Phillips and Mike Phillips - An insightful look into the Windrush saga, emphasizing the social and cultural impact of the generation on Britain.

"Black and British: A Forgotten History" by David Olusoga - This book sheds light on the rich history of Black people in Britain, going back to Roman times and weaving through the Windrush era to present day.

"Innovate or Die: Outside the Square Business Thinking" by Andrew Grant - A tome that's vital for understanding the importance of innovation in achieving economic success and generational wealth.

"Family Wealth: Keeping It in the Family" by James E. Hughes Jr. - A deep dive into the nuances of creating and maintaining generational wealth, with practical steps and family stories.

Documentaries and Films

"The Windrush Generation: Empire of Dreams" - A documentary that provides a visceral visual narrative of the journey and struggles of the Windrush pioneers.

"Britain's Forgotten Slave Owners" by David Olusoga - A powerful, revealing documentary that examines the role of Britain in slavery and its lasting effects on modern society.

Online Resources

Black Cultural Archives - A rich resource for anyone looking to explore the history of Black people in Britain. (*https://www.bcaheritage.org.uk/*)

The Windrush Foundation - An organization dedicated to preserving the history and contributions of the Windrush Generation. (*http://www.windrushfoundation.com/*)

Embracing our past, acknowledging the present, and innovating for a prosperous future is a journey we can all participate in. These resources are just the beginning. They serve as a beacon, guiding the way towards a deeper understanding, appreciation, and application of the principles that have been covered in this narrative. As we look to the stories of those who came before us, let their courage, creativity, and tenacity inspire us to forge our own paths to success and fulfillment.

Remember, the legacy of the Windrush generation is not just a chapter in history; it's a living, breathing inspiration that continues to influence and shape our world. Let's honor that legacy by seeking knowledge, challenging barriers, and building bridges toward a future where generational wealth and well-being are attainable for all.

Acknowledgments

The creation of this book has been a journey as enlightening as it is enriching, threading through the ebbs and flows of history to paint a portrait of perseverance and triumph that embodies the Windrush generation. In the process of weaving this narrative, a multitude of individuals and organizations have generously contributed their insights, stories, and support, without which this work would not have reached its fullest potential. It is with profound gratitude that I acknowledge their contributions.

Firstly, I must extend my heartfelt thanks to the countless individuals of the Windrush generation and their descendants. Their willingness to share personal narratives and experiences has been the backbone of this book, offering authenticity and depth to the critical examination of generational wealth and prosperity amidst adversity. These stories have not only illuminated the past but also shone a light on the path forward, inspiring hope and determination in future generations.

To the historians, scholars, and researchers whose tireless work laid the groundwork for this exploration, I am deeply indebted. Their invaluable insights into the socio-political and economic landscapes that shaped the experiences of the Windrush generation have allowed for a nuanced understanding of the complexities involved in building a legacy of wealth that transcends generations.

I also owe a great deal of appreciation to the community organizations that have preserved the cultural heritage of the Windrush era. Through their dedication, they have ensured that the memories and achievements of this pivotal generation remain alive, offering a wealth of resources and knowledge that has greatly enriched this book.

A special acknowledgment must also go to my editorial team, whose meticulous attention to detail and unwavering support guided this project from a mere concept to the comprehensive exploration that lies within these pages. Their expertise and encouragement have been paramount in bringing this story to light.

Finally, to you, the readers, who embark on this journey through history with an open mind and heart, seeking to understand and apply the lessons of the past to build a brighter, more prosperous future. This book is for you, a beacon of hope and a testament to the enduring power of innovation, creativity, and resilience. May the legacy of the Windrush generation inspire you to chart your own course toward fulfillment and success, in wealth and wellbeing alike.

As we stand on the shores of history, looking back at the voyages undertaken by generations before us, let us also gaze forward with optimism and ambition, propelled by the lessons they have taught us. Together, we can build on the foundations laid by the Windrush generation, striving for a future rich in opportunity, diversity, and prosperity for all.

About the Author

Dr. Sonia Michelle Reynolds embodies the indomitable spirit and unwavering determination that characterized the Windrush generation. Born to Jamaican immigrants Nerva and Ezra Reynolds during the Windrush era, Sonia's upbringing was steeped in the ethos of hard work, resilience, and entrepreneurial ingenuity.

From a young age, Sonia witnessed the tireless efforts of her parents as they balanced multiple jobs to make ends meet. Her mother, a dedicated nurse by day, would spend her evenings stitching together knitted panels to create woollen jumpers. Her father, a skilled bricklayer, would sell these garments to his colleagues on the building site. The warmth and appreciation these jumpers brought to their recipients left an indelible mark on Sonia's heart, igniting her passion for business and creativity.

Fuelled by her parents' entrepreneurial spirit, Sonia pursued her dreams with unwavering determination. She earned a 2:1 degree in knitted textiles from Derby University, laying the foundation for her journey as a businesswoman. With the support of the Prince's Youth Business Trust, she launched her first venture in exclusive quality knitwear, which quickly gained international acclaim.

When faced with challenges, Sonia pivoted her skills to interior design and real estate investing, navigating new avenues of opportunity with grace and resilience. Her ventures flourished, providing her with the means to pursue her passion for innovation and research.

Driven by a thirst for knowledge and a desire to make a difference, Sonia embarked on a PhD journey, exploring novel methods of fabric manufacturing. Her groundbreaking research has garnered multiple awards, secured numerous patents, and forged partnerships with global companies.

Beyond her entrepreneurial pursuits, Sonia is deeply committed to serving her community. For over two decades, she has dedicated her time and expertise to empowering individuals within the local Black British Caribbean and Christian community, inspiring them to achieve their educational, personal, and professional aspirations.